CW01658556

ECONOMICS IN MINUTES

NIALL KISHTAINY

BOARD OF TRADE MARKETS
RYE
BARLEY
FLAX
BARLEY
CLEAR BELLIES
LARD
RYE
WHEAT
CORN
OATS
NEW
BONDED

ECONOMICS IN MINUTES

NIALL KISHTAINY

Quercus

CONTENTS

Introduction

What makes some societies richer than others? Why do banks crash? How high should taxes be? These are questions that economists try to answer, but often disagree about. To the layman, economics can seem an obscure language – one filled with jargon and complicated mathematics. And economic news can be bewildering, as share prices soar and crash, and the economy lurches from crisis to crisis. In fact, underneath the specialist terminology, much economics comes down to some fairly simple principles. This book will give you a flavour of theories about how the economy works and how it should be managed.

What actually is economics? The term was used by the Ancient Greeks and comes from a Greek word meaning 'management of the household'. Nowadays, economics encompasses much more than this, but households and individuals have always been building blocks of the economy. People make decisions about what to buy with their incomes and how much to work. In doing this they encounter a basic economic fact of life: resources such as food, electricity or time are limited and choices have to be made about what to consume and what to produce. It is people who make these choices, so explanations of human behaviour are a central part of economics – what makes a consumer buy a new computer, a businessperson build a factory, and a worker accept a job in a far off city?

Most economists think of their subject as a science: they try to uncover general laws that govern economic phenomena, such as trends in unemployment – just as physicists look for laws that explain the acceleration of a rocket. But finding laws of human behaviour is much harder than explaining the path of a rocket. This is why economists disagree so much, for example on whether the government should spend more money to pull the economy out of recession, or on the levels at which public debt is sustainable. This book demystifies the complex vocabulary in which these debates are conducted, boiling down economic concepts into accessible explanations that will hopefully make the important and influential ideas of economics easier to understand.

Economic man and rationality

At its core, economics is a theory of human behaviour. Economists see people as rational beings that respond with consistency and logic to economic variables such as prices and interest rates, and even to things like the weather, which can affect the economy. What this boils down to is that people make decisions in a way that maximizes their economic pay-off – they will always buy the car or coat that is exactly in line with their preferences, at the lowest price possible.

Economics' version of rationality requires people to be able to gather and assess information – for example, the prices and characteristics of different goods – and to then calculate the best decision with ease. In reality, far from being cold, rational calculators, people are often capricious and emotional, and may at best make economic decisions that are 'good enough' or based on plausible rules of thumb rather than a thorough reckoning. Nevertheless, economists see rationality as a useful simplification and use it as a basis for most of their theories.

CARS

Scarcity

Resources are finite – at any point in time there is only so much wheat, coal or cement to go around. Resources can be used in myriad ways: cement could be used to build new homes or renovate factories, wheat may be processed into various foods and consumed by different people. New houses, better factories and more nutrition are all worth having, but because resources are finite, we cannot have them all: how to choose between them is a fundamental question of economics.

Economists see the problem in terms of trade-offs: competing options each have costs and benefits, but the best will be that which maximizes overall benefits over costs. The analysis of the trade-offs inherent in allocating scarce resources is the essence of modern economics: British economist Lionel Robbins described it as 'the science which studies human behaviour as a relationship between ends and scarce means which have alternative uses'. Economists have come to believe that the market offers a powerful way of deciding between these uses.

AEON

Utility

Economics posits an underlying logic to human behaviour: whether it be a purchase of food or a choice about savings, all decisions are aimed at maximizing 'utility'. If I prefer strawberries to bananas I am said to gain more utility from strawberries than bananas, perhaps quantified as a utility of 'four' compared to 'two'. Maximization of utility is the sole aim of rational economic man, and while economics is often thought of as the study of money, money is simply needed to buy things, and the utility generated is the driver of behaviour.

Utility is subjective: strawberries add to my well-being but reduce that of someone who dislikes them. Early theories saw utility as a scale like money: someone with a utility of four was twice as happy as someone with a utility of two. But because it is impossible to directly observe, economists now think of it as a ranking – we can say someone gains more utility from strawberries than bananas because we see his choice, but cannot really measure how much absolute utility they provide.

Preferences

Economics views well-being in terms of the extent to which a person's preferences – his or her desires for one thing rather than another – are satisfied. But because resources are scarce, there is a limit to the extent to which people's preferences really can be satisfied. Individuals experience this in facing a 'budget constraint': they can only sate their desires up to the amount of money that they have to buy goods. In doing so they are said to maximize their utility or well-being.

Of course, it is hard to observe a person's full set of desires, and for this reason economists tend to think in terms of what they call 'revealed preference': if we see a person spending her money on jeans when she could have afforded a skirt then we infer that she prefers jeans to skirts. From this starting point, economics attempts to explain how individuals respond to a loosening or a tightening of their budget constraint as a result of changes in prices and incomes.

Jeans
Skirt
Dress

Opportunity cost

In everyday thinking, the cost of going to a university consists of tuition fees plus the cost of food, rent and so on. Economists instead prefer to think of the true cost of choosing one option as the opportunity which had to be given up as a result: so in this example, the opportunity cost of going to university is getting a job. The biggest cost of university is likely to be the money that could have been earned, and many of the direct outlays made by a student – food and rent – would still need to be made in employment and might even cost more.

The concept of opportunity cost helps to determine if resources are being put to best use. Suppose that a firm bases its operations in a building that it owns in the centre of town. It may pay no rent for its offices, but may be giving up the opportunity of earning a large rental income by leasing out the centrally located building and locating its staff in a cheaper suburban building.

Substitutes and complements

Different kinds of chocolate bars are what economists call substitutes – they all satisfy the same basic want, so that if the price of one bar increases, people will buy less, and buy more of another kind instead. In contrast, some goods are consumed jointly, compact discs and CD players, for example. If the price of compact discs rose, the demand for CD players would fall. Economists call these kinds of goods complements.

Many goods are of course unrelated – in the sense that when the price of one changes, the demand for the other is unaffected (tuna and computer games, perhaps). Goods may have degrees of substitutability and complementarity: for example, two brands of orange juice may be substitutable, but butter and margarine are less so. Substitutability is considered by competition authorities when they assess the extent to which a firm might be monopolizing a market: a firm controlling the butter market would be less able to raise prices if consumers could switch to margarine.

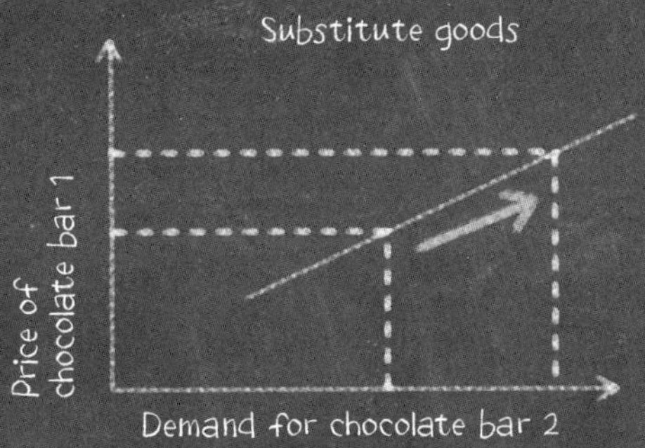
Substitute goods
Price of chocolate bar 1
Demand for chocolate bar 2

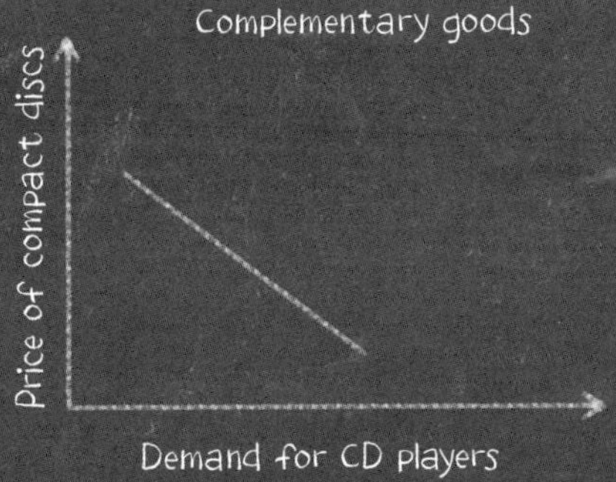
Complementary goods
Price of compact discs
Demand for CD players

Normal and inferior goods

Suppose you get a pay rise. Feeling richer, you increase your consumption of your favourite beer. In this case, the beer is what is known as a normal good: consumption of it rises with income, and if your income fell you would consume less of it.

But now you are richer, you also drink less of that cheap brand of cider you used to consume. In this case, the cider would be an inferior good – you consume less of it as your income rises, more of it when poorer. Luxury goods like caviar or sports cars can be thought of as a special type of normal good for which consumption increases by proportionately more than income when income rises.

Of course, a good may sometimes be normal and sometimes inferior depending on the level of a consumer's income. If I get a pay rise I might drink more beer, but if I then win the lottery, I might ditch the beer completely and only ever drink champagne.

Income and substitution effects

Picture a student who spends his money on nothing but chips and cola – then, because of a bumper potato harvest, the price of chips falls. This affects the student's spending in two ways. Firstly, the price of cola in terms of chips has risen: for every can of cola the student buys he has to give up more chips than before. He buys less cola but more bags of chips. This is what economists call the substitution effect. Secondly, because chips are cheaper, the student's purchasing power has risen – in a sense his income is now larger. He may well decide to buy both more chips and more cola. This is the income effect.

Economists break down changes in demand as a result of price changes into these effects. The overall impact on the student's consumption of chips is clear: both the income and the substitution effects point towards him buying more. But the impact on his consumption of cola is ambiguous: the substitution effect means he buys less but the income effect makes him buy more.

Consumer surplus

While a woman is out shopping, she sees exactly the right-sized wardrobe for her bedroom. She would be willing to pay £250 for it, but the price is just £100. As a result, the woman enjoys a consumer surplus of £150 – the difference between what she would be willing to pay and what she actually pays.

At very high prices, only a few of these wardrobes would be sold to those with high 'willingness to pay'. At a price of £100, those individuals gain a large consumer surplus, but if a total of 500 wardrobes sold across the whole market is ranked by surplus, the 500th will be sold to someone willing to pay exactly £100 – for more to be sold the price would have to be lower, inducing people with a 'willingness to pay' below £100 to buy one. Adding up the consumer surplus of each buyer gives us the total consumer surplus across the entire wardrobe market. Economists believe this is a measure of economic well-being: when it is high, consumers' desires are being satisfied well.

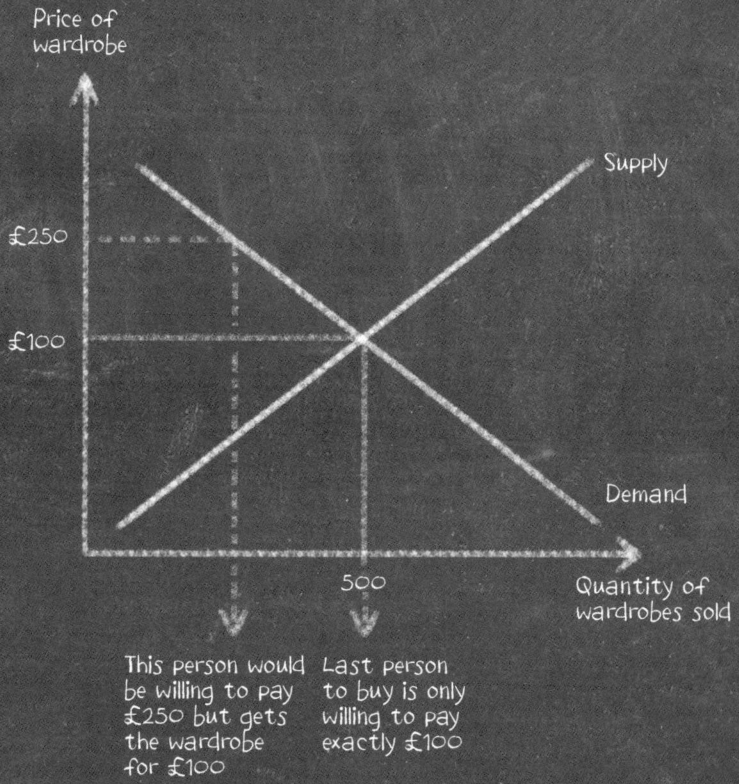

Price of wardrobe
Supply
£250
£100
Demand
500
Quantity of wardrobes sold
This person would be willing to pay £250 but gets the wardrobe for £100
Last person to buy is only willing to pay exactly £100

Engel's law

The 19th-century German economist Ernst Engel identified a basic pattern in the relationship between food expenditure and income. He argued that as income rises, people increase their spending on food by a smaller amount, so the proportion of income allocated to food falls. Someone tripling their income overnight would be unlikely to triple their consumption of food, unless they had started off in poverty.

The law implies that the poor spend a higher proportion of their income on food – very poor families living in developing countries often spend most of their income on basic staples. Contrast this with a consumer in a rich nation, whose income is spent on a complex basket of goods – housing, travel, holidays, entertainment – within which food may be just a modest share. Engel's law highlights the vulnerability of the poor to increases in the cost of food – if most of their income goes on food, they may not be able to adequately feed themselves when prices rises.

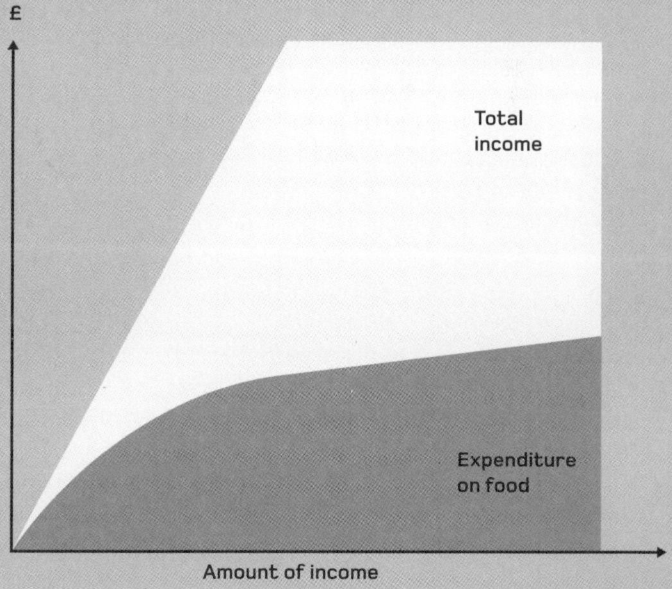
£
Total
income
Expenditure
on food
Amount of income

Time and discounting

Economic decisions are not just about whether to buy, but *when* to. If I am impatient, I may borrow money to buy a television today. If I am patient, however, I will wait until I have earned the money myself. Economists call people's level of impatience their time preference. Although some are more patient than others, in general people prefer a television today to a television in a month. People are said to 'discount' the future.

People who discount at a high rate are likely to save less, and consume more today. This is related to the idea of an interest rate. £100 in a year's time is viewed as worth less than £100 today, so if I lend someone £100, I will ask for more than £100 to be returned to me in a year. If I expect to receive £100 in one year, then I would want to know the 'present value' of this amount. This would be the amount that I would have to lend out at interest today to be paid back £100 in a year, and would be less than £100.

TODAY
1 YEAR LATER
100
110

Labour supply

Decisions about how much to work can be thought of as a choice between consumption and leisure. How does a worker respond to an increase in her wages? Intuitively one might think that she would work more: an hour of leisure has become more costly in terms of the wages lost, and therefore the consumption that she must give up, so she takes less leisure time and works more.

But with a higher wage, the worker has become richer: she can afford more leisure, and so may therefore work less. It is possible that the second effect might outweigh the first, in which case the overall effect of the higher wage has been to make the worker work less. And this outcome is not just a theoretical possibility: over the last couple of centuries the length of the working week in the industrialized world fell even as wages were rising considerably. As workers got richer, they used their greater wealth to take more leisure.

The paradox of value

Why is it that a glass of water, so vital to life, is worth hardly anything, whereas a diamond, which has no practical use, is so valuable? This is the so-called paradox of value, discussed by philosophers and economists down the ages, and perhaps most notably by the 18th-century Scottish economist Adam Smith. The paradox can be resolved with the concept of 'marginal utility'.

Utility is the pleasure or well-being from the consumption of a good such as a grape (see page 12). Marginal utility is the pleasure that is gained from an extra unit of consumption, so if I eat five grapes the marginal utility is the extra pleasure I received from the fifth grape. Marginal utility tends to decline: the fifth grape probably gave me less extra utility than did the first. Because diamonds are so scarce, their marginal utility is very high and they therefore have a high value. In contrast, because water is readily available in most parts of the world, the marginal utility of an extra drop is much lower.

Supply and demand

In a free market, the price of a good is determined by supply and demand. The market price of wheat emerges through the interaction of the supply of wheat by farmers and the demand for it from flour mills and food manufacturers: when the level of supply is equal to the level of demand the market is said to be in equilibrium.

In equilibrium, the market is at rest, because all the mills wanting to buy wheat at the prevailing price can find a farmer willing to sell some, and all the farmers wanting to sell wheat can find a flour mill willing to buy some. Often, however, markets get thrown out of equilibrium: perhaps a sudden drought lowers wheat supply below demand, leading to a shortage. The power of the free market is in its ability to correct this: because there are too many mill owners chasing too few bushels of wheat, farmers can increase their prices without losing sales. The higher price chokes off demand and stimulates supply, until the market returns to equilibrium.

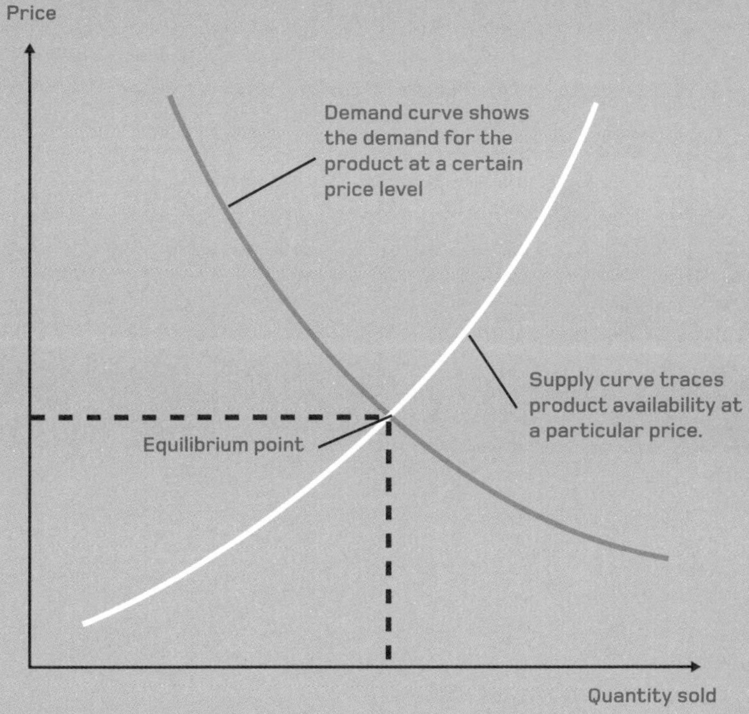
Price
Demand curve shows the demand for the product at a certain price level
Supply curve traces product availability at a particular price.
Equilibrium point
Quantity sold

The law of demand

A basic 'law' of economics is that when the price of a good rises, people demand less of it, and when the price falls people buy more. Although this prediction is a fairly robust one, like any law stated in the abstract, assumptions are used that may not always hold up in practice. For example, a showroom slashing the price of its cars might lead to queues around the block. But what if people were unsure about the quality of the cars? A lower price might signal that the cars were of low quality, leading to fewer not more buyers.

In addition, there are other factors beyond the price of a good that can affect demand for it: consumer tastes might alter or changes in the price of goods that are close substitutes for it might affect demand. There are some special kinds of goods, such as goods which are consumed in order to display one's wealth (so-called conspicuous consumption, see page 360) for which demand may actually *increase* when the price goes up.

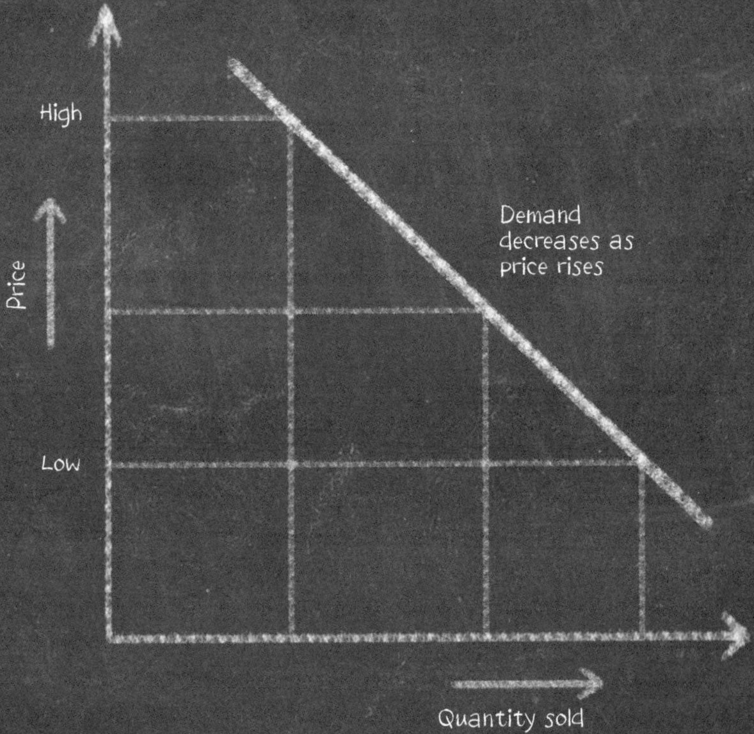
High
Low
Price
Demand
decreases as
price rises
Quantity sold

Elasticity of demand

People respond differently to changes in prices for different goods. Suppose, for example, that the price of jam rises: consumers might easily switch to marmalade, leading to a fairly large fall in the demand for jam. Demand for jam is thus sensitive to changes in prices – what economists call elastic demand. In contrast, consider a village only served by a single bus: a rise in the bus fares might not affect demand very much. Here bus travel is said to be *price inelastic*.

Goods that are necessities, or those for which there are few substitutes, tend to be inelastic, while those that are luxuries or are easily substitutable tend to be elastic. In the short term, demand tends to be more inelastic, but over time consumers may adjust to price changes. In the 1970s, the oil-producing countries attempted to keep the price of oil high to earn themselves large revenues. In the long run, however, consumers reduced their demand for oil by switching to more fuel-efficient cars.

Giffen goods

If the price of laptops increases, one would expect people to demand less of them. However, economic theory also allows that a price increase might generate more, rather than less, demand. A price increase has two effects that may contradict each other: a higher price makes consumers shift spending towards other, cheaper goods, but in addition, the price increase reduces consumers' purchasing power, cutting real income. Some goods, such as laptops, tend to be demanded less when income falls. Another category of good known as inferior goods are demanded *more* as income falls. 'Giffen goods' are inferior goods with such a strong income effect that when the price goes up overall more of the good is demanded. Poor households spending most of their income on a basic staple suffer a large fall in real income if the price of the staple rises. Households may respond by cutting out non-essential items like meat or sugar, and spending even more on the staple. Some have claimed that during the Irish famine of the 19th century, potatoes were such a Giffen good.

Paradoxically, demand for a Giffen good rises as its price increases, since this reduces consumers' ability to spend on alternative goods.

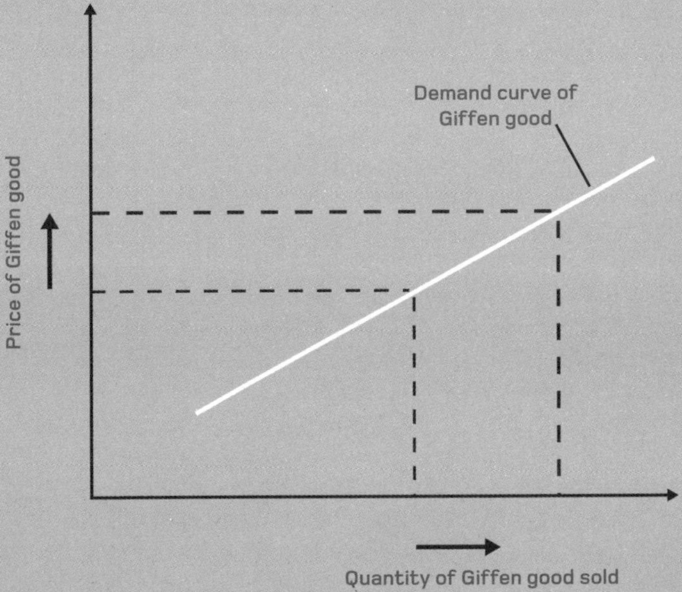

General equilibrium

If the price of petrol rises, consumers tend to demand less of it. They may use their cars less and buy bicycles, and as a result, the price of bicycles rises and resources shift towards the manufacture of bicycles as new producers enter the market. In this way different markets are connected, and a shock in one may ripple through the rest.

Often we tend to think of markets in isolation: we talk about the price of cars that brings supply into line with demand: what economists call partial equilibrium. *General* equilibrium theory considers the possibility of equilibrium across the whole economy, taking account of the linkages between markets. One might imagine that completely unfettered free markets would lead to muddle and instability – why would one expect that any kind of order would arise? General equilibrium theory has shown that under certain conditions there are prices that bring about equilibrium in all markets. However, whether these conditions actually hold in practice is another matter.

The invisible hand

In the 18th century, Scottish economist and philosopher Adam Smith famously wrote: 'It is not from the benevolence of the butcher, the brewer, or the baker that we expect our dinner, but from their regard to their own interest.' If I am hungry, the butcher supplies me with meat and in buying it from him I provide him with his living.

The 'invisible hand' was Smith's metaphor for the way in which free markets spontaneously satisfy people's wants. No coordinating organization orders the butcher to supply meat at a particular spot, or tells the hungry person to turn up there for his dinner. Supply is made equal to demand by prices, so that everyone who wants to buy something at that price can obtain it. A fundamental tenet of much of economics is therefore that the result of people acting purely in their own self-interest will not be chaos, but rather social good. Much deep economic thought is concerned with the way in which the invisible hand works, and the conditions in which it might fail.

Pareto efficiency

Economists want to do more than just explain economic outcomes: they also want to assess how desirable they are. The standard they apply is Pareto efficiency, named after the Italian economist who devised the concept.

Suppose Tom has two packets of crisps and two packets of sweets. He likes crisps, but is indifferent to sweets. Jane has two packets of crisps, and likes both crisps and sweets. If Tom gave Jane the sweets, she would be better off and he would not be worse off: this would be a Pareto improvement. The original allocation of goods was 'Pareto inefficient' because they could be reallocated to make someone better off without hurting anyone else. When all such reallocations are made, society achieves Pareto efficiency, the state in which it is not possible to make anyone better off without hurting someone. Market exchange takes place when both buyer and seller stand to gain, and much of economics is concerned with uncovering the conditions in which free markets lead to Pareto efficiency.

From any point along the Pareto efficiency curve it is impossible to make one person better off without hurting the other.

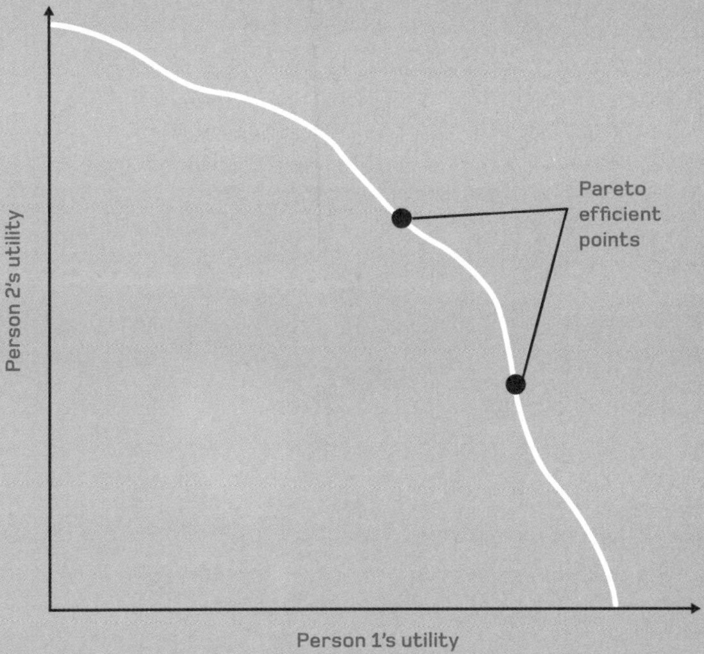

Market efficiency and the welfare theorems

Adam Smith claimed that a system of free markets spontaneously leads to a socially desirable allocation of goods (see page 44). Without any central organization, the right goods and services get produced and end up in the hands of those who can put them to best use. It's as if all the buyers and sellers, workers and employers are guided by an 'invisible hand'. In the 20th century, economists investigated this idea mathematically, deriving 'welfare theorems' that set out conditions under which free markets lead to social good.

Their criteria for social good was Pareto efficiency (see page 46): an allocation is said to be Pareto efficient if no further reallocations of goods can be made to benefit at least one person while hurting no one. One of the welfare theorems states that under certain conditions any allocation of goods arrived at through the action of free markets is Pareto efficient. The catch is that the conditions are so stringent that they are unlikely to hold in the real world.

Market failure

Under certain conditions, markets can give rise to efficient allocations of goods (beyond which it is impossible to make a person better off without hurting someone else). When such conditions are not met, market failure arises. One condition for efficiency is competition: no buyer or seller should be able to influence the price of a good. So one market failure is lack of competition: if a monopoly controls the bread market, it can raise the price and supply less, creating an inefficiency. Another efficiency condition is that a market outcome only affects those participating in it: your purchase of a bunch of bananas doesn't affect me, but suppose you buy a drum kit, forcing me to wear earplugs? Your action had an unintended consequence that was not taken into account in the price you paid for the drums. Economists call this kind of failure an 'externality'.

Market failure is used to justify government intervention: for example, so-called 'anti-trust' policy deals with monopolies, while certain kinds of taxes can be used to offset externalities.

An important aim of public policy is to correct market failures

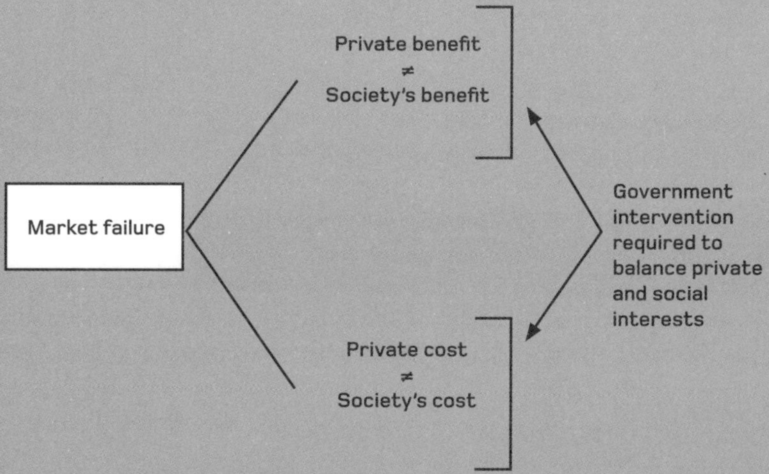

Externalities

Suppose a car factory is located upriver from a fishery. The factory buys materials and labour, sells its cars and turns a profit. But a by-product of its production is a chemical that is released into the river. It flows down to the fishery and kills some fish. The impact of the chemical on the fishery is an externality: the factory creates a cost to the fishery that is not taken into account of in the market. When the factory decides how many cars to make it looks at the cost of materials and the price of cars – the lower output of fish doesn't enter into it. So the market has failed to bring the costs and benefits faced by the factory into line with those for society as a whole: the 'negative' externality can be seen as the factory producing 'too many' cars. Conversely, markets have a tendency to undersupply 'positive' externalities. Bees pollinate crops, but the beekeeper only considers the price of honey, not the benefit from his bees to the neighbouring farmer. Relative to the potential benefit overall, the beekeeper has 'too few' hives.

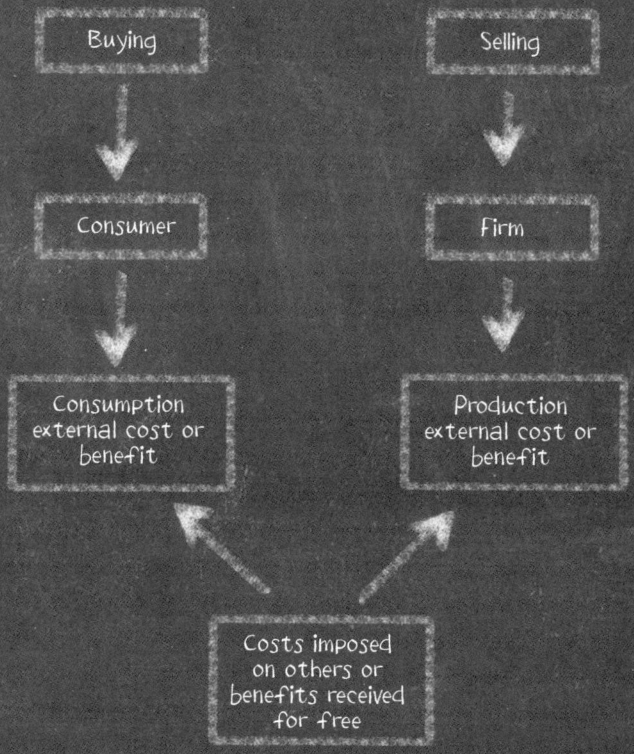
Buying
Selling
Consumer
Firm
Consumption external cost or benefit
Production external cost or benefit
Costs imposed on others or benefits received for free

The tragedy of the commons

Picture a traditional village in which people make a living from the sale of wool, grazing their sheep on a collectively owned common pasture. The village prospers and more sheep are put to graze. But soon there are so many sheep that the grass is eaten faster than it can grow back. Eventually, the ground is bare and no sheep can be supported on it – the villagers' livelihood disappears.

This 'tragedy of the commons' comes about because when individual owners graze their sheep, they don't take account of the fact that this reduces the grass available to other villagers' sheep. Here the grass is a common resource: no one can be excluded from using it, but one person's use reduces that for others. The combined effect of the villagers' actions is self-defeating – if they could agree to limit the number of sheep, perhaps using taxes or quotas, their livelihoods could be protected. This is what lies behind governments' attempts to regulate common resources such as water, roads and fish.

The Coase theorem

Suppose that John takes up the trombone and his neighbour Jack can't stand the din. The trombone gives pleasure to John, but imposes a cost on Jack. This cost isn't reflected in the market and so John isn't made to face the full cost to society of his hobby. Economists say that John creates a negative externality. In 1960, economist Ronald Coase proposed a theorem suggesting that markets can solve the problem.

Suppose that the pleasure from the trombone is worth £1,000 to John, and the annoyance to Jack is equivalent to £2,000. Jack could pay John £1,500 to stop playing. Both John and Jack are made better off. This assumes that John had an initial right to play the trombone. It could be that Jack has the right to peace and quiet, in which case John could attempt to pay him to allow trombone playing. In either case, the theorem says that parties should be able to bargain their way to a solution. In reality, however, the theorem might not work: bargaining is often too costly to bring a solution.

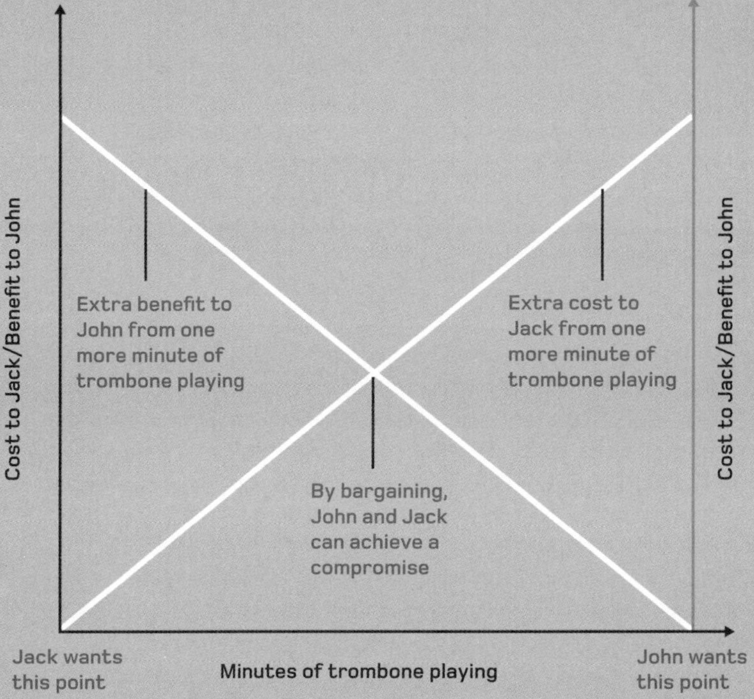
Cost to Jack/Benefit to John
Extra benefit to John from one more minute of trombone playing
Extra cost to Jack from one more minute of trombone playing
By bargaining, John and Jack can achieve a compromise
Cost to Jack/Benefit to John
Jack wants this point
Minutes of trombone playing
John wants this point

Public goods and free riding

Ten residents of a street each place a value of $100 on the installation of streetlights: overall, they would get a benefit of $1,000. So if the cost of the lights was less than $1,000, it would be beneficial to install them, with each resident contributing to the cost.

But streetlights are a special kind of good known as a public good: no one can be excluded from using them, and one person's use does not reduce their availability to others. Why, then, would a resident admit to valuing streetlights at all and contributing to their installation? It would be more rational for him to feign indifference, knowing that once the streetlights were installed he would still benefit because he couldn't be excluded from their use. If all the residents 'free ride' in this way, no contributions are made and the streetlights don't get installed. Free riding means that markets cannot supply public goods: one of the main roles of government is to invest in socially beneficial public goods such as national defence.

The second best

Economists espouse the benefits of free, well-functioning markets. When a market fails, then the first response is often to propose that an intervention should be made to correct the problem. The theory of the second best shows that the situation is more complex.

Suppose we were worried about a firm monopolizing the steel market. Monopolies tend to drive up prices and restrict output compared to the social ideal, so we might suggest intervention from an 'anti-trust' agency to break the firm into smaller competitors: steel output would rise and prices would fall. But suppose there is another market failure: the firm pumps gases that damage nearby crops. The firm doesn't take account of this cost – if it did it would produce less steel. So one market failure – lower output arising from the monopoly – offsets the other failure of pollution costs arising from overproduction. Correcting just one failure – the monopoly – might worsen the situation, because even more crops would be damaged.

2

Arrow's impossibility theorem

In any society, some people might want extra resources to go to schooling, and others may want it spent on roads. When making collective decisions, societies must grapple with the problem of such conflicting desires. Arrow's impossibility theorem shows that logically there is no procedure for making such decisions that simultaneously satisfies a small number of reasonable criteria for fairness. One of these properties is that there is no 'dictator': no single person who determines society's decision. Another is that if *every* individual preferred schools to roads, then society as a whole should prefer schools to roads. The theorem states that these, and other apparently sensible criteria for fairness, are inconsistent.

Consider a voting system that met the second condition: as a result there would be a dictator – a single vote would always determine the outcome. The theorem is powerful and disturbing: even the most transparent voting systems are likely to be bedevilled by inconsistency and paradox.

YOUR
VOTE
COUNTS

Risk and uncertainty

Economic life is imbued with risk. A trader's portfolio might lose value or go through the roof, a worker might be laid off or get a raise. Risk refers to situations in which there are a set of known events that will occur with measurable probabilities, such as the different outcomes on a roulette wheel.

Much economic analysis uses this idea: firms and individuals calculate expected returns from different courses of action and then choose the one with the highest return. For example, a firm believes with a high probability that there will be large market demand next year: it therefore decides to launch a new product. Uncertainty refers to situations in which future events do not have a known probability and so expected returns can't be calculated. Uncertainty pervades all economies: for example, it is impossible to know what new kinds of technologies might exist a decade from now. This means that in reality a great deal of economic decision-making about the future is driven by hunches rather than calculations.

Risk aversion

Suppose I offer to give you £1,000 if a coin toss comes up heads, but nothing if it comes up tails. Because both heads and tails outcomes occur with a probability of one in two, we can say that the expected value of the coin toss is £500. Knowing this, suppose that I now give you a choice between taking the gamble or receiving £490 immediately?

According to economics, if you take the £490 you are said to be risk averse: you are willing to accept a lower pay-off in order to avoid a risky gamble in which you may end up with nothing. This is because the pain of a loss exceeds the pleasure of a gain: you would probably refuse to play a game in which I paid you £100 if a coin came up heads, but you paid me £100 if it came up tails. Risk aversion explains the existence of insurance markets: risk-averse individuals pay a premium to an insurer each year to avoid the possibility of facing a larger loss.

Insurance

Sophie buys household insurance, and yet she has never been burgled. Why does she continue to pay? She does so essentially because she seeks to avoid risk. With insurance she ends up with less wealth in the event that she doesn't get burgled, but if she is burgled, the insurance company makes up the losses. Insurance transfers wealth from the outcome in which she is not burgled to the one in which she is. Without it, she will end up with a higher return in the first outcome, a lower return in the second. The expected returns – wealth in each outcome weighted by the probability of the outcome – are the same with or without insurance, but still, because she hates risk she takes out the policy. The company, meanwhile, can insure her by insuring large numbers of people: it is hard to predict whether Sophie herself will be burgled, but one can make a reasonable prediction about how many out of 1,000 people will be. The company can therefore ensure that the total premiums paid will cover the total amount paid out.

The principal–agent problem

Markets may not work properly when some people have more information than others. For example, the owner of a building firm wants to maximize his profits, but this depends on the efforts of his employees. This is known as the principal–agent problem: an outcome that is important to the owner (the principal) depends on the actions of the workers (the agents). However, the agents have more information than the principal about their own actions. The owner of the building firm can't monitor the effort of all the bricklayers and carpenters scattered across various building sites.

Much economic theory looks at the question of how the principal can create incentives for agents to act in the way he wants, when these actions are costly to the agents. Other examples of principal–agent problems occur in health markets: the principal (the patient) may be concerned about whether her doctor is recommending a beneficial treatment or merely one that is profitable to him.

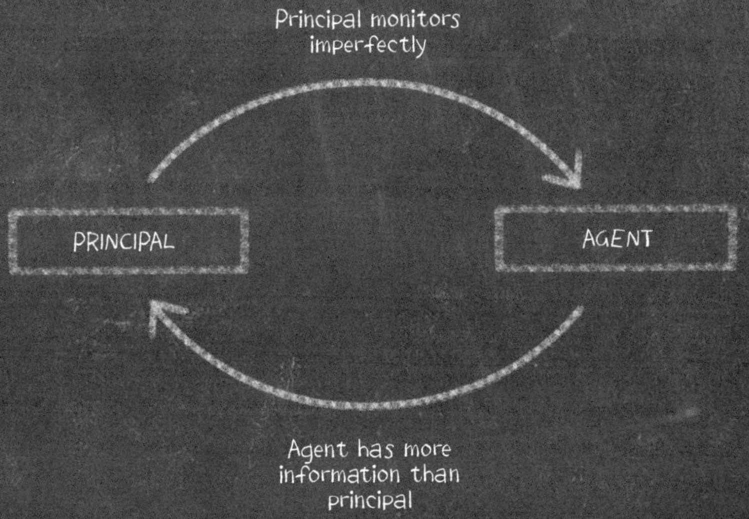
Principal monitors imperfectly
PRINCIPAL
AGENT
Agent has more information than principal

Moral hazard

Dave insures his mobile phone, and knowing that he is now covered for any damage by the insurance company, he begins to treat his phone rather carelessly, claiming the costs of fixing various breakages. This situation, in which Dave is able to affect the probability of the event (phone damage) under which the insurance company pays out, is an example of moral hazard. The problem in this case is that the insurance company cannot monitor each of its customers and may end up paying out more than expected: if it could it would charge higher premiums to careless people like Dave. But because it can't, the company charges higher premiums for everybody. It may even stop selling certain kinds of insurance. The firm's lack of information hobbles the market.

Many economists have claimed moral hazard contributed to the financial crises that began in 2007: if banks are considered 'too big to fail' they may take on overly risky investments, knowing that they will be bailed out by government later on.

Adverse selection

Consider the case of a stallholder selling cheap perfume – his willingness to sell at this price raises suspicions that the perfume may be fake. The problem arises because unlike the seller, the buyer is uninformed about the quality of the perfume. In this situation of 'adverse selection', the market tends to push out sound products in favour of bad ones.

To take another example, the condition of a second-hand car may be unknown to the buyer, but owners of duds have more incentive to sell than owners of sound vehicles and so buyers expect that the average quality of cars on offer is low. As a result, they are only willing to pay low prices, and because owners of sound cars can't get decent prices, fewer of these are offered until eventually only duds are left. Adverse selection also arises in health insurance where people's health is unknown to the insurer. Those most keen to buy insurance may be the unhealthy ones that the insurer least wants to insure.

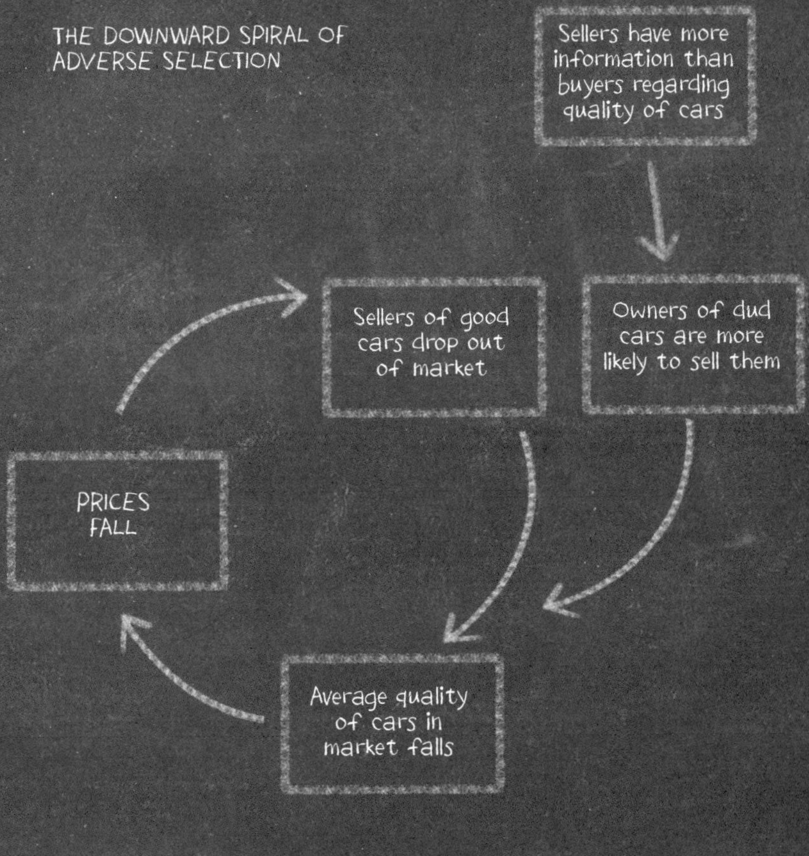
THE DOWNWARD SPIRAL OF ADVERSE SELECTION
Sellers have more information than buyers regarding quality of cars
Owners of dud cars are more likely to sell them
Sellers of good cars drop out of market
Average quality of cars in market falls
PRICES FALL

Signalling and screening

Markets don't function well when some people have less information than others, but one theory suggests that informed participants can sometimes 'make a signal' that reveals information to solve the problem. For example, firms wish to hire productive workers, but it is hard for firms to observe these characteristics. Workers are aware of their own capabilities and can signal these abilities by gaining qualifications. Suppose that an accountancy firm awards a training contract to a history graduate over an applicant without a degree. The graduate's studies were unrelated to accountancy and the firm plans to train her in the discipline from scratch, but the degree has acted as a signal of valued characteristics – diligence and ability. If the firm was able to directly observe ability levels, the degree would be redundant. Uninformed parties can also take actions, known as screening, to make others reveal information about themselves. Insurance companies and lenders ask potential customers questions that are designed to reveal how risky they are.

Auctions and the winner's curse

At an auction, Jane is the winning bidder for an antique clock and pays £50.00 for it. She wins because her bid is higher than all the other bids, but this means that in some sense she paid 'too much' for the clock – a phenomenon known as the winner's curse. If the second-highest bid was £49.00, then Jane would still have won the clock with a bid of £49.01 and so has ended up paying 99 pence more than she needed to.

The analysis of auction strategy has become an important part of economics. One important question concerns the best bidding strategy – might Jane have done better to slightly lower her bidding limit to reduce the probability of paying too much, or would she have risked losing the auction? Another question is how the seller of an item should design auctions to maximize revenue. This gained prominence in the 1990s, when governments sold off radio spectrum rights to mobile phone operators. Insights from auction theory were used to design auctions that maximized returns from the sales.

Searching and matching

In the standard model of markets, prices are what bring demand into line with supply. In the labour market, the number of people who want to work at the going wage should equal the number that employers wish to take on. In reality, however, workers don't know about all the jobs and salaries available. Acquiring information about job opportunities is costly in terms of time and research, so workers will search for a job until they find a good match – one that fulfils their preferences at an acceptable wage. But because search is costly it is rational for them to limit the amount of time they spend searching and to accept a wage that is 'high enough', even if there may be higher-paid jobs available. These costs mean that a range of wages can be found for the same job, rather than a single one. They also explain the phenomenon of 'frictional unemployment' – the unemployment that exists even in booming economies simply because of the time it takes for workers to find new jobs.

Game theory and the prisoners' dilemma

The branch of economics that considers strategic decision-making is known as game theory, and the prisoners' dilemma is perhaps its best-known example. Two thieves are captured, questioned separately and urged to give evidence against each other. They know that if both stay silent they will receive a light sentence of a year in prison. Alternatively, if one of them betrays their partner and the other stays silent, the former is released and the latter will be sentenced to 20 years. If both betray, however, they will each get 10 years. Since the worst outcome is clearly to get double-crossed, they both end up betraying each other and receive 10 years each. But by acting rationally the thieves have missed out on the best outcome – that of mutual silence. An economic example of a prisoners' dilemma is a cartel – a group of firms that agree to restrict output to keep prices high. Given high prices, it is rational for a firm to produce more to reap large additional profits, but when all firms do this, output shoots up and prices collapse, undermining the cartel's original aim.

Prisoner 2 \ Prisoner 1	Confess	Keep silent
Confess	Both jailed for 10 years.	Prisoner 1 jailed for 20 years. Prisoner 2 walks free.
Keep silent	Prisoner 1 walks free. Prisoner 2 jailed for 20 years.	Both jailed for 1 year.

Credible threats

In many markets, a small number of firms compete and their individual outputs affect prices. In making decisions, therefore, firms must take into account the reactions of competitors. They may try to influence them with threats, but these only work if they are credible.

Consider CemOld, a monopoly supplier of cement that earns large profits through high prices by underproducing. NewCem now considers entering the market and CemOld knows that this would drive down prices. So it threatens to boost production in the event of NewCem's entry, hitting the profits of both firms. CemOld hopes this will deter the newcomer, but if NewCem does enter the market it would not be rational to carry out its threat: it is not credible. A threat can be made credible by showing commitment to it – CemOld could invest in a new factory, and having made that outlay, it will need to produce cement from the new plant. This could make it profitable to raise output significantly if NewCem do enter.

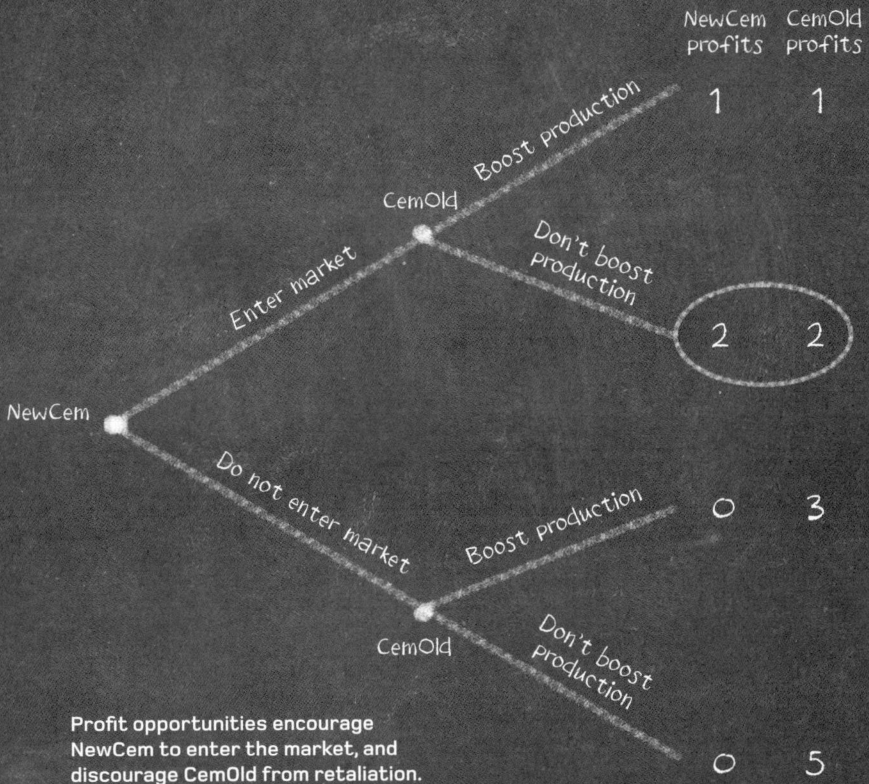

Profit opportunities encourage NewCem to enter the market, and discourage CemOld from retaliation.

Behavioural economics

Economists often think of consumers and firms as rational, in the sense that they choose actions that maximize benefits over costs, but observation of people's choices shows this is far from the way people actually behave. The new branch of behavioural economics studies these quirks.

For example, standard economics posits that people have a consistent attitude to risk – often they are risk averse, tending to prefer certain safe outcomes to riskier but more profitable ones. Behavioural economics has shown that people behave differently when facing potential gains or losses – with gains they seem risk-averse, but facing loss they appear risk loving, taking on risk to avoid potential losses. It seems that people hate losing a certain amount more than they like to gain it. One implication of this is the 'endowment effect': people place a higher value on a car that they already own than one they see in the showroom. Rational economic man would have a single valuation of the car, regardless of whether he owned it.

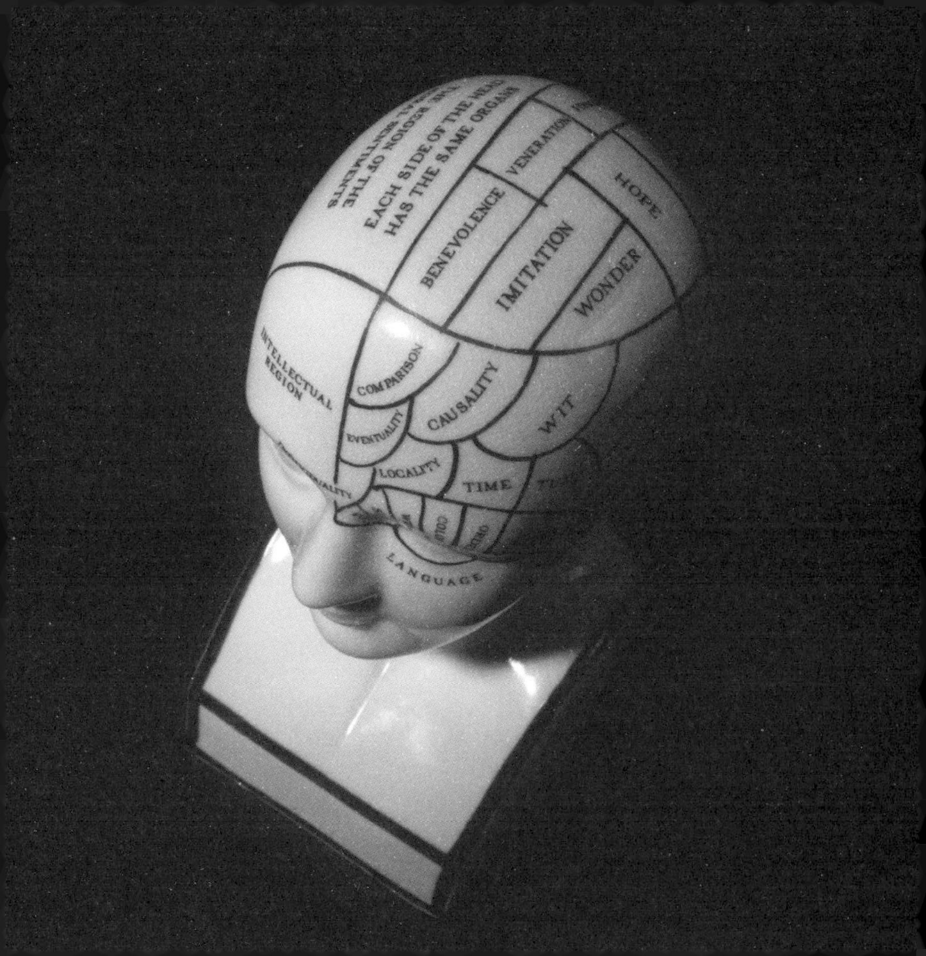
EACH SIDE OF THE
HAS THE SAME ORGANS
BENEVOLENCE
VENERATION
HOPE
IMITATION
WONDER
INTELLECTUAL REGION
COMPARISON
CAUSALITY
WIT
EVENTUALITY
LOCALITY
TIME
LANGUAGE

The Allais paradox

French economist Maurice Allais gave his name to a paradox in which economic behaviour violates a basic notion of rationality. Suppose that Sally can choose between a Mars Bar or a Twix, and chooses the Mars Bar. She is then offered a choice between a Mars Bar, a Twix and a Snickers. If she is economically rational, she should choose either the Mars Bar or the new option, the Snickers; the addition of a Snickers to the range of options shouldn't change her preference for the Mars Bar over the Twix.

Economists call this criterion of rationality 'independence'. But in more complex situations where people were expected to choose between uncertain outcomes, Allais found that independence would frequently be violated: somehow people were influenced by the inclusion of alternatives that should have made no difference. Allais's insights have prompted economists to investigate more closely the psychological bases of economic behaviour.

The role of money

A person's overall wealth may consist of houses and paintings, a portfolio of shares, a fat bank account and sackfuls of cash. But only some of these assets are money – those which can be routinely exchanged for goods and services. What is it that distinguishes money from paintings or houses? Money is first a medium of exchange. Societies that do not have money face a problem known as the 'double coincidence of wants': if I want to buy a loaf of bread and have a piece of meat to give in exchange, then I need to find someone with bread who happens to want meat at the same time. Money solves this problem.

Money is also a unit of account. Wages, loan repayments, the prices of wheat or computers are all measured in the same comparable units. When a baker sells a loaf of bread, he earns a pound that he can use later on to buy a newspaper: money therefore acts as a store of value, and it has been central to the emergence of modern economies.

2000
BANCA D'ITALIA
200 duzentos cruzeiros
2 REAIS
10 REAIS
TEN
नेपाल राष्ट्र बैंक
中国人民银行
壹角
THE UNITED STATES OF AMERICA
IN GOD WE TRUST
ONE
NARODNA BANKA SRBIJE
10
20
REPÚBLICA POPULAR DE MOÇAMBIQUE
CEM METICAIS
100
BANK NEGARA MALAYSIA
1000 LIRE MILLE
México
DE ESPAÑA
MIL PESETAS
1000
BANCO ESPAÑOL
KRONOR
50
10000
NARODNA BANKA
KUNA
CENTRALNA BANKA BOSNE I HERCEGOVINE
ЦЕНТРАЛНА БАНКА БОСНЕ И ХЕРЦЕГОВИНЕ
10
КОНВЕРТИБИЛНИХ МАРАКА
CENTRAL DE LA ARGENTINA
CINCO MIL PESETAS
5000
FEDERAL

Fiat and commodity money

So-called commodity money has intrinsic value aside from its monetary value: early forms of money such as gold coins were of this type. Commodity money is costly because it ties up the valuable raw materials used to make it. It is also vulnerable to debasement – mints have an incentive to reduce the precious metal content. The amount of commodity money in circulation also depends on the availability of the commodity – for instance, the economy can be flooded if new metal reserves are found.

Fiat money is a more sophisticated kind of money that avoids these problems – $100 bills and electronic balances are not tied to any underlying commodity: they are money simply because society agrees that they are. When properly managed by a responsible government, fiat money enables monetary policy – the manipulation of interest rates and money supply in order to manage the economy (see page 248). The risk, however, is that profligate governments can print excessive amounts of money, leading to hyperinflation (see page 220).

Money in modern economies is in the form of intrinsically worthless notes. In earlier societies it was made out of precious metals.

Money supply

The money supply is the overall level of monetary assets in an economy. A variety of different kinds of assets can act as money, so the money supply is made up of various components, depending on how different economists or statistical bodies choose to define it.

Reference is often made to 'narrow' or 'broad' money. Narrow money is made up mainly of the most tangible forms: notes and coins. In developed economies, however, the main component of the money supply is the stock of money in bank accounts, and broader definitions of the money supply can include bank deposits in current and savings accounts. As financial systems become more complex they offer a greater choice of money-like assets. This means that precise control of the money supply by the authorities can be difficult. Different forms of money are sometimes denoted by the terms M0, M1, M2, M3 and M4 from narrow to broad, although once again, organizations may define these categories in different ways.

Money supply in New Zealand, 1988–2008

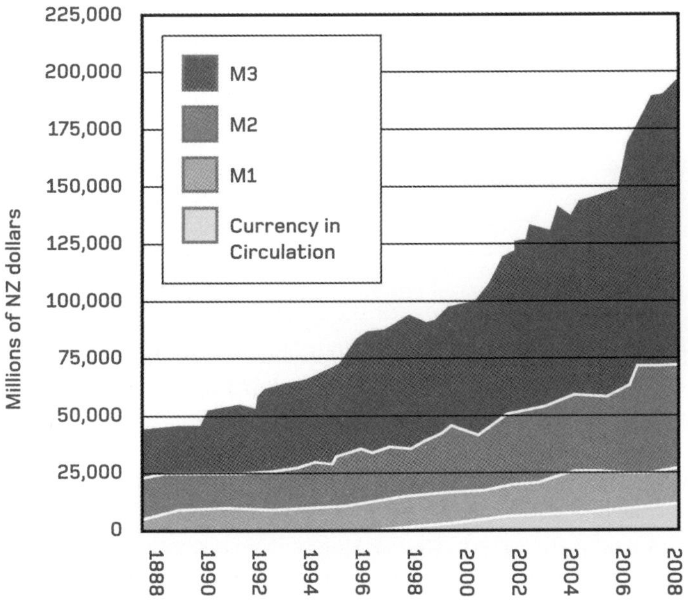

Money creation

Banks hold only a fraction of their deposits as cash, and this 'fractional-reserve' system is used to create money. Suppose that a bank has $1,000 of deposits, contributing $1,000 to money supply. The bank holds just $\frac{1}{10}$ of its deposits as cash reserves: it keeps $100 and lends out $900. Savers still have deposits totalling $1,000, but borrowers have $900, an addition to the money supply on top of the original $1,000. The economy is no richer in real terms – the borrowers eventually have to pay back the $900 – but there is now a greater stock of money for use in transactions. When borrowers spend their $900, it ends up with another bank, which keeps a fraction of it as cash before lending out the rest, and so on.

A 'reserve ratio' of $\frac{1}{10}$ eventually generates a money supply of $10,000 from the original $1,000. The lower the ratio, the more money that is generated. Governments try to control money supply by influencing this process – for example, by changing interest rates or by restricting the reserve ratio.

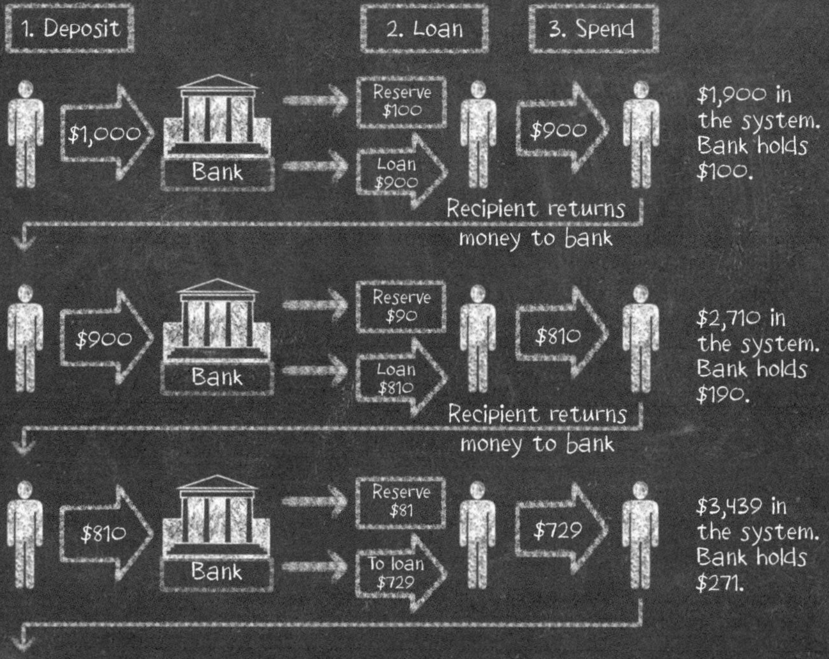
1. Deposit
2. Loan
3. Spend
$1,000
Bank
Reserve $100
Loan $900
$900
$1,900 in the system. Bank holds $100.
Recipient returns money to bank
$900
Bank
Reserve $90
Loan $810
$810
$2,710 in the system. Bank holds $190.
Recipient returns money to bank
$810
Bank
Reserve $81
To loan $729
$729
$3,439 in the system. Bank holds $271.

The demand for money

People can hold their wealth in various forms such as money, shares, property and other assets. Just as we talk of the demand for apples or houses, we can also consider the demand for money. People choose to hold their wealth as money – to demand it – for several reasons. They need money to carry out transactions, to buy food and pay bills, but uncertainty about the future also causes people to hold money to cover unforeseen expenses. The more transactions that need to be carried out, the more money people will demand. So as economies grow, the demand for money tends to increase.

Money – in particular cash – does not pay interest so by holding onto it one forgoes the potential returns from financial assets such as bonds. When the interest rates on offer are higher, one gives up more by holding money, so the demand for money tends to fall as interest rates rise. Inflation in prices also decreases the demand for money, because its purchasing power is reduced.

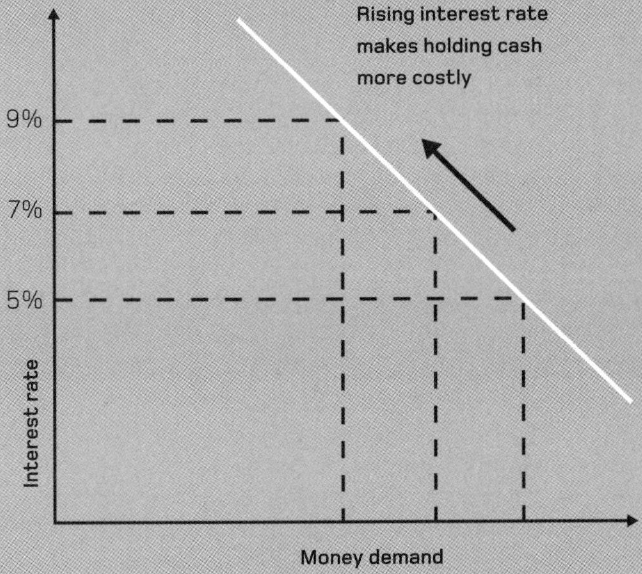
Rising interest rate
makes holding cash
more costly
9%
7%
5%
Interest rate
Money demand

Interest rates

Interest is paid to holders of financial assets such as bonds. The rate of interest is determined by the supply and demand for money. When rates are high people buy interest-earning financial assets; they are less willing to hold money, while when national income is higher, people need more money for transactions. Suppose the central bank sets a certain level of money supply. The money market comes to rest when demand for money is equal to supply, and for this to happen, the interest rate must adjust to the level at which people are willing to hold an amount of money equal to that supplied by the central bank.

Suppose the central bank now floods the economy with money. Given national income, people don't need that much money to trade. At the current interest rate they don't wish to hold all this extra money, so in order for them to keep hold of it interest rates must fall: bonds become less attractive and people become willing to hold the extra money supply, returning the market to balance.

Seigniorage

Governments have a monopoly on the production of money, and the cost to the authorities of printing a bank note is a fraction of that note's value. The revenue that this creates for the government is known as seigniorage and, along with taxation and borrowing, it is a method by which the state can raise finance. This is what happens when governments finance spending by printing money rather than by borrowing or raising taxes.

But, in fact, seigniorage functions as a sort of tax – printing money raises the money supply and pushes up inflation, so seigniorage can be thought of as an 'inflation tax' because higher prices reduce the real value of people's money. As with any tax, the government boosts its own purchasing power at the expense of everyone else's. Although seigniorage can be a useful source of revenue it can also be dangerous: if it is taken to an extreme it can lead to hyperinflation (see page 220).

Money illusion

Unlike gold coins, modern money – in the form of cash and bank deposits – has no intrinsic value. A note is worth $10 only because society agrees it is. What you can buy with it depends on prices. Money illusion happens when people confuse money's nominal value – a note's face value of $10, for example – with its real value – the amount of goods and services that it can be used to buy.

Suppose a worker is paid $100 per week: her nominal wage. If she spends all her money on books and the price of books doubles, then her real wage has halved. However, people seem to take more notice of changes to their real wages caused by changing nominal wages than those caused by changing prices: they balk more at a 10 per cent cut in nominal wages than at an equivalent rise in prices with an unchanged wage. Some economists have suggested that during times of inflation, workers supply more labour than they otherwise would because they think their wages are higher than they really are.

When the price of books is high...

$100 =

When the price of books is low...

$100 =

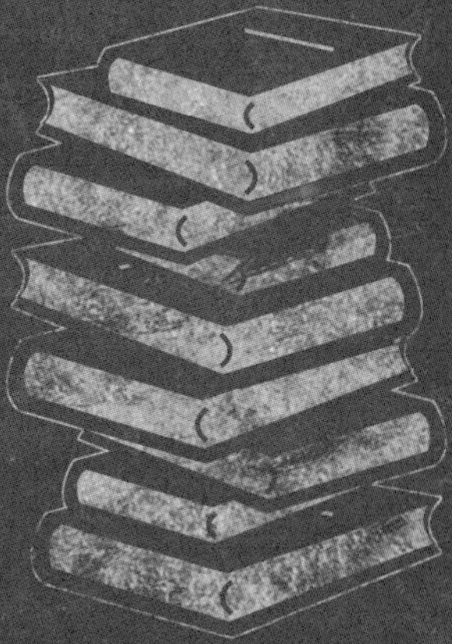

The Fisher effect

Named after US economist Irving Fisher, the Fisher effect refers to the impact of inflation on nominal interest rates, and the difference between nominal and real rates. Suppose you earn 10 per cent interest on a bond each year – how much this return is worth (in terms of what you can actually buy with it) depends crucially on the rate of inflation. If inflation had been 4 per cent then your real return would be only 6 per cent.

From this, one can see that the 10 per cent nominal interest rate can be divided into a real interest rate and the rate of inflation: the nominal rate is equal to the real interest rate plus inflation. If inflation rises by 1 per cent – perhaps because of an increase in the supply of money – then nominal interest rates should also rise by 1 per cent. Studies of trends in interest rates and inflation over time appear to confirm the Fisher effect: high inflation rates and high interest rates seem to go together.

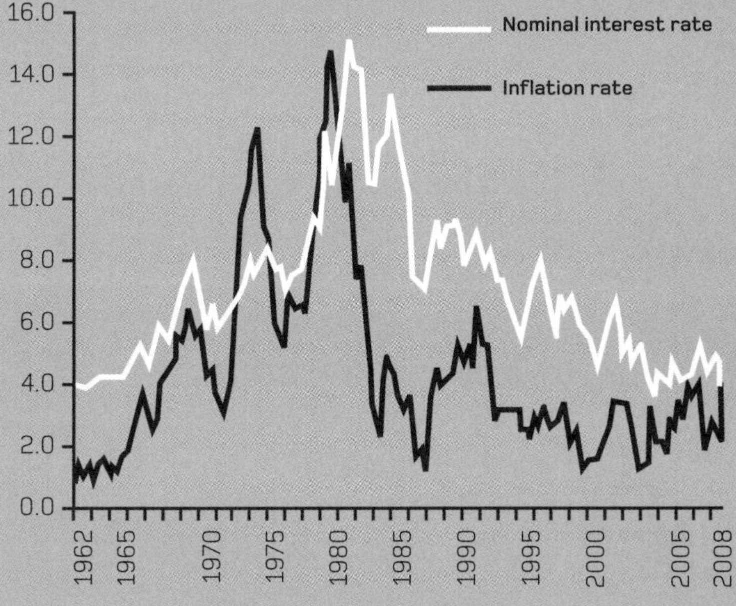

Trends in US inflation and interest rates appear to confim the Fisher effect.

Banks and financial intermediation

National income can be consumed today or invested in projects that promise future returns. Investments in infrastructure, factories, technology and skills all drive growth and so investment is the lifeblood of economies. So banks – in the role of financial intermediaries connecting savers with investors – are an important artery for investment. People who don't consume all of their income today save it, depositing it in banks from where it is channelled to those who wish to use money to carry out investment projects.

Banks are able to pool savings from many people and then transform them into loans. By dealing with many savers and borrowers, they are able to manage risks. An important part of this involves balancing the interests of borrowers and savers: savers might want immediate access to their funds, while borrowers carrying out large investment projects require long-term loans. Poor management of the various risks can disrupt the mechanism of financial intermediation.

Bank runs

Typically, banks keep only a small percentage of deposits as cash, which they can use to pay immediately to depositors making withdrawals. Banks need to judge the prudent level of deposits to keep as ready cash, balancing this with the need to earn profits by lending the money to borrowers. A bank run happens when depositors believe that the bank is no longer able to pay them back their money.

Bank runs create their own momentum and can even be self-fulfilling: this is due to the fact that banks operate on the assumption that only some borrowers will want to withdraw their money in a given period. If borrowers come to doubt the bank's ability to pay them back, they will all rush to withdraw simultaneously and then the bank really won't be able to pay them. This is why many governments insure bank deposits in the hope that this will short-circuit the cycles of panic that have the potential to sink otherwise healthy banks.

FOURTH
NATIONAL
BANK

Bonds

Borrowers can get loans from savers through financial intermediaries such as banks. But they can also gain direct access to savers through financial markets such as the bond market. Suppose that Mega Foods Inc. wants to build a new plant. It can raise funds by selling bonds that are, in essence, IOUs. John's purchase of a bond from Mega Foods Inc. is a loan to the company – the bond states a date of maturity at which John's loan will be repaid, along with a rate of interest that will be paid until then. John can hold onto the bond until it matures or sell it on earlier. Governments also issue bonds to finance expenditure.

Bonds vary in how long they take to mature – short-term bonds may mature in a matter of months, while long-term bonds may run for decades. Some bonds are more risky – those for which there is a higher probability that the firm or government might not make its repayments. Risky borrowers need to offer higher interest rates on their bonds in order to raise finance.

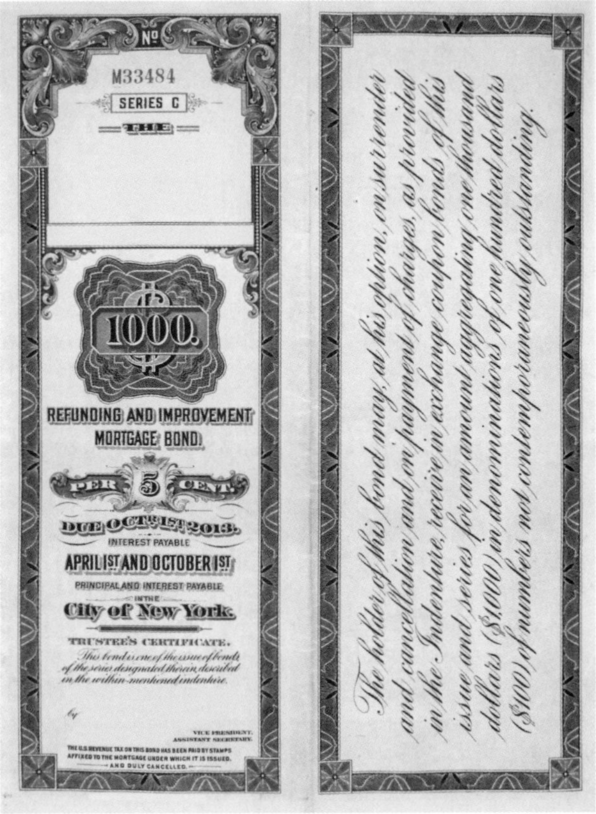

US railroad bond, c.1900

Risk and return

Risk and return go together: risky financial assets or investment projects tend to offer higher potential returns in the future, and when risk is low, potential returns are also likely to be low. Because people tend to avoid risk but like high returns, risk and return form a trade-off: to get higher potential returns, one has to take on more risks.

Imagine that a firm starts producing a novel product: it is hard to predict whether the product will catch on and the firm will survive, and for this reason, an investor lending to the firm would demand a high rate of interest. If the product did well and the firm made huge profits, its shareholders would make a lot of money and the people who'd lent it money would receive their hefty interest payments. But conversely, the firm might also end up going bust, in which case investors would lose out. At the other extreme, one could invest in safe government bonds: these have a very low risk of default but pay low rates of interest.

Risk and return for different forms of investment

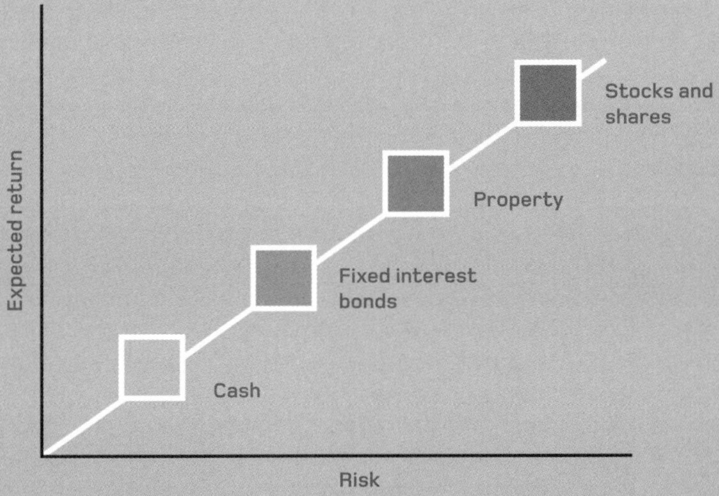

The stock market

One way for firms to raise finance directly from investors is by selling shares (stock). When an investor purchases a share in a company, she owns a share of the firm. This form of finance contrasts with debt financing from the issuing of bonds: bondholders have lent money to a firm, while shareholders actually *own* the firm. As a result, investing in shares is relatively risky but offers a high potential return – if the firm does well it may pay out some or all of its profits in the form of a dividend on each share, and its share price will also rise – in both ways, its shareholders become richer. But if it goes bust, shareholders lose their investment completely. In contrast, bondholders receive the same interest payments even if the firm's share price hits the roof. The trading of shares takes place on central stock markets like the London Stock Exchange. Once a firm has issued shares they can be sold on by investors. Companies' share prices rise and fall depending on firm performance. Stock prices are also affected by the overall state of the economy.

BOARD OF TRADE MARKETS
RYE
BARLEY
FLAX
BARLEY
CLEAR BELLIES
LARD
RYE
WHEAT
CORN
OATS

The capital asset pricing model

The capital asset pricing model (CAPM) is a method of calculating the expected return on an investment based on risk. An asset has two kinds of risk – specific and systematic. Specific risk affects a particular investment – for example, the potential fall in the share price of a pharmaceutical company whose flagship drug has been found to be harmful. This kind of risk can be offset by diversifying investments across many companies. Systematic risk is that which affects the whole market (for example, when the economy enters a recession and all stock prices fall) and cannot be offset by diversification.

Broadly speaking, the CAPM says that the expected return on an asset is related to the expected return on the stock market as a whole. Some assets move closely with the overall market: they have a high degree of systematic risk that can't be diversified away and therefore a high expected return. Other assets have lower systematic risk and so usually offer lower returns.

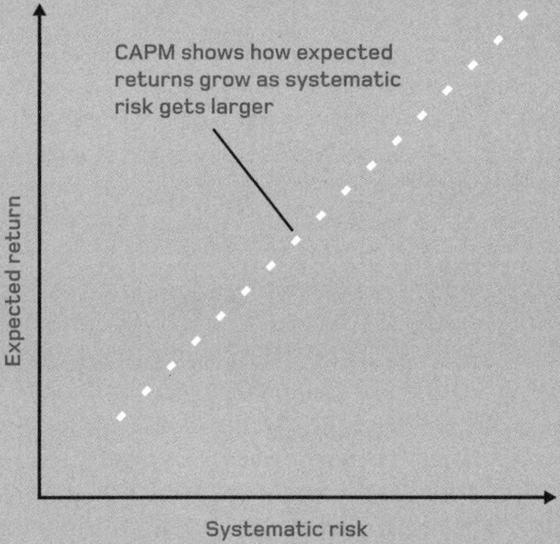
CAPM shows how expected returns grow as systematic risk gets larger
Expected return
Systematic risk

The yield curve

When the rates of returns on debt of varying periods are compared, the resulting graph gives the relationship between short- and long-term interest rates, known as a yield curve. Normally, the curve slopes upwards: returns rise with the borrowing period; in other words, long-term interest rates are higher than short-term ones. Suppose an investor lends the government £100 by buying a bond. The government pays him interest and returns the money in six months. If the repayment period was three years, one might expect a higher interest rate. By lending for longer, the investor takes on more risk: in three years many unforeseen events could occur.

Sometimes, the yield curve slopes downwards: short-term rates exceed long-term ones. This indicates that investors expect short-term interest rates to fall (otherwise one could borrow at the long-term rate to re-lend at the short-term one). Expectations of falling short-term rates can be a sign that an economy is about to enter a downturn.

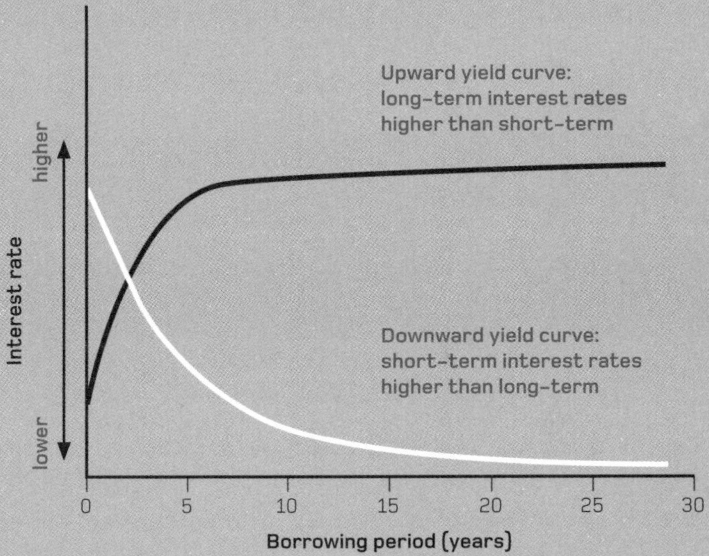
Upward yield curve:
long-term interest rates
higher than short-term
Downward yield curve:
short-term interest rates
higher than long-term
Interest rate
higher
lower
0
5
10
15
20
25
30
Borrowing period (years)

Financial engineering and derivatives

Financial derivatives have been around for centuries, but have grown in importance and sophistication in recent decades. Derivatives are contracts that involve an underlying commodity such as wheat or dollars – for example, a contract could specify a price and future date of delivery for 100 tonnes of barley. These kinds of contracts are particularly useful for managing risk: they can reduce uncertainty about future prices. But this feature of derivatives also allows speculators to make money. Suppose I buy a derivatives contract for the delivery of 100 tonnes of barley in six months for £100 per tonne. If the actual price of barley in six months is £120 tonnes per tonne I can make a profit of £20 per tonne by immediately selling on the barley. In recent decades, highly complex derivatives have been devised using mathematical models to price the risk inherent in different kinds of contracts. Some have blamed the recent economic crisis on this kind of 'financial engineering', which introduced financial products so complex that few understood them.

Tobin's Q

In 1968, economists James Tobin and William Brainard put forward an argument for a link between investment and the stock market. Tobin devised a measure showing this connection, which came to be known as Tobin's Q.

Suppose that a firm is considering making an outlay on some new capital stock. It could do this by issuing new shares on the stock market (see page 116). If the price of its shares is greater than the cost of the extra capital stock then the firm should make the investment. One can think of a share price as reflecting the market's valuation of the firm's capital, so if it is high relative to the cost of installing extra capital then the firm should make the outlay. Tobin's Q is the total market value of a company divided by the cost of replacing its capital stock. When Q is high, investment should be high – in particular, when Q is greater than one the firm is 'overvalued': its market value is higher than the replacement cost of its assets, which should encourage it to invest in more capital.

$$\text{Q ratio} = \frac{\text{total market value of company}}{\text{total asset value}}$$

The efficient markets hypothesis

According to the idea of market efficiency, the price of a stock, or any other good, should reflect all the information relevant to valuing it (see page 118). The efficient markets hypothesis suggests that it is therefore impossible for an investor to consistently 'beat' the market. In fact, if financial markets are really efficient, one might as well invest in a random selection of stocks. Investors constantly monitor the fortunes of companies and watch out for new information that may affect their values. They make money by buying the shares of undervalued firms and selling those of overvalued firms. In efficient markets, price brings supply into line with demand: those who want to buy a stock at a certain price should exactly balance those who want to sell it, and therefore stock prices are always a good indication of the value of a firm. The hypothesis is called into doubt by the fact that markets often seem irrational, with herd behaviour leading to bubbles and crashes. Recent crises have shown that markets don't always take all information into account in an efficient manner.

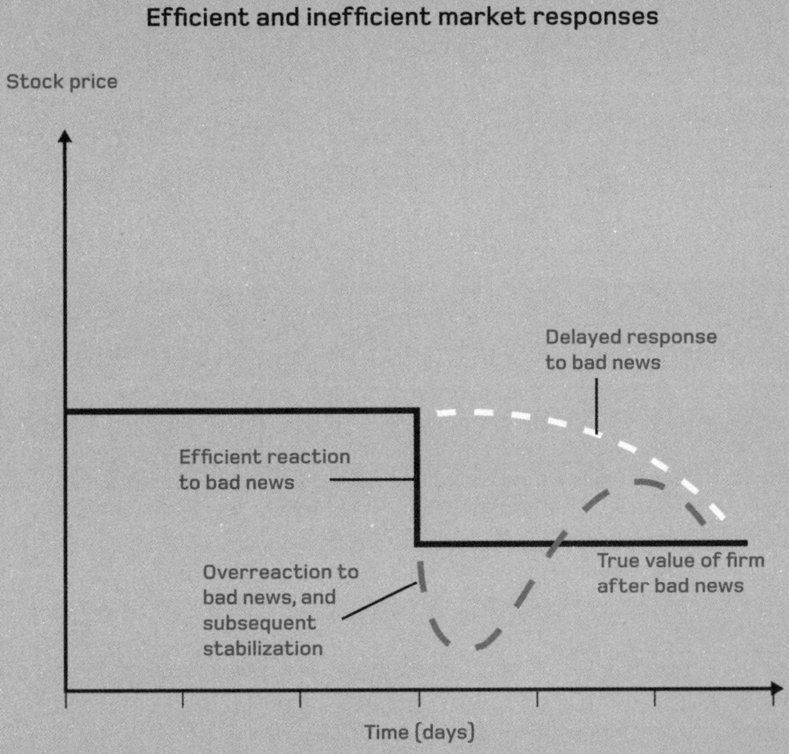
Efficient and inefficient market responses
Stock price
Delayed response to bad news
Efficient reaction to bad news
True value of firm after bad news
Overreaction to bad news, and subsequent stabilization
Time (days)

Financial crises

There are many kinds of financial crisis. The recent global crisis has led to the revival of an an idea put forward in the 1960s by Hyman Minsky, who argued that economic stability inevitably gives rise to instability and crisis. With sustained economic growth comes confidence in the future: people borrow money to invest in assets such as houses, and as confidence grows they may take on greater risk – they might take out larger loans and only pay back the interest, anticipating that the value of their assets will rise.

In the run-up to the crisis of 2008, generous lending was fuelled by a growing market for financial securities based on mortgage loans. As a result, loans were issued to many homebuyers who were at a high risk of defaulting on their payments. Eventually, the behaviour encouraged by widespread confidence leads to instability – a so-called 'Minsky moment'. When the US housing market began to decline many borrowers couldn't repay, leaving lenders with huge debts and triggering the crisis.

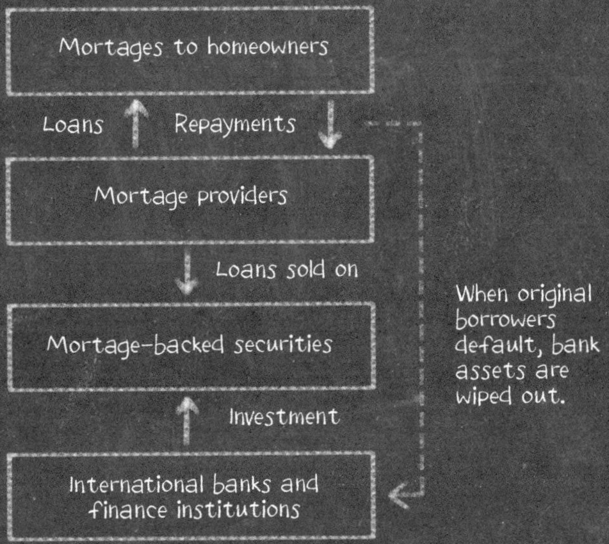

Circumstances leading to the financial crisis of 2008

Credit crunches

Credit fuels economic activity: firms have to borrow to invest in factories or research new products, individuals take out loans to buy houses or to finance education. So when credit dries up the economy gets smothered. During a credit crunch, the supply of loans contracts: there is both less credit available and a tightening of the conditions for accessing it.

Credit crunches often arise from certain kinds of market failure. For example, at the start of the recent economic crisis in 2008, financial institutions realized that loans had been given to homebuyers based on a limited analysis of their creditworthiness, and that many were in fact worthless. To reduce their risks, they immediately began to restrict credit to borrowers. Much of this behaviour is driven by so-called 'informational failures': when it becomes apparent that there is not enough information about the true risks attached to a bank's stock of loans, the response can be to switch from liberal to highly conservative lending policies.

Financial bubbles

Like a bubble, prices of assets such as stocks or property can sometimes seem to rise ever upwards. Prices often rise for good reason, but during a bubble the price rises above the fundamental value of the asset. Bubbles are an example of economic irrationality – people stop making decisions based on the true value of an asset but instead follow the herd. They buy the good – technology stocks in the early 21st century, tulips in the 17th – merely because they see that other people are buying it and believe that they will be able to sell it for a higher price in the future.

At first the prophecy is self-fulfilling – enthusiasm for the good pushes up the price and soon more investors join in a collective frenzy of buying, leading to an increasingly inflated price. Eventually, however, the process stalls and the market crashes. People seem to think that prices will go on rising forever, or at least that they will eventually be able to sell on their asset to someone who *isn't* able to foresee the bursting of the bubble.

During the Dutch 'tulip mania' of the 17th century, the price of some flowers exceeded many workers' annual incomes.

Financing firms

Traditionally, a firm can raise money through borrowing or through selling shares (equity). The Modigliani-Miller theorem states that the way in which a firm finances itself has no bearing on its value. The idea is that when markets are efficient and investors rational, all that matters is the profit that a firm makes, and it is this alone that determines its value.

One of the authors of the theorem explained it using the analogy of a firm as a vat of whole milk. The farmer could sell the whole milk (corresponding to pure equity financing – the sale of shares). Alternatively, the farmer could separate out the cream and sell this at a higher price (analogous to the firm financing itself through borrowing). However, just as skimming cream off the whole milk leaves less valuable skimmed milk, so borrowing makes the firm's shares less attractive, offsetting any gain. Like the farmer deciding the split between cream and skimmed milk, the firm does just as well whatever combination of debt and equity it decides on.

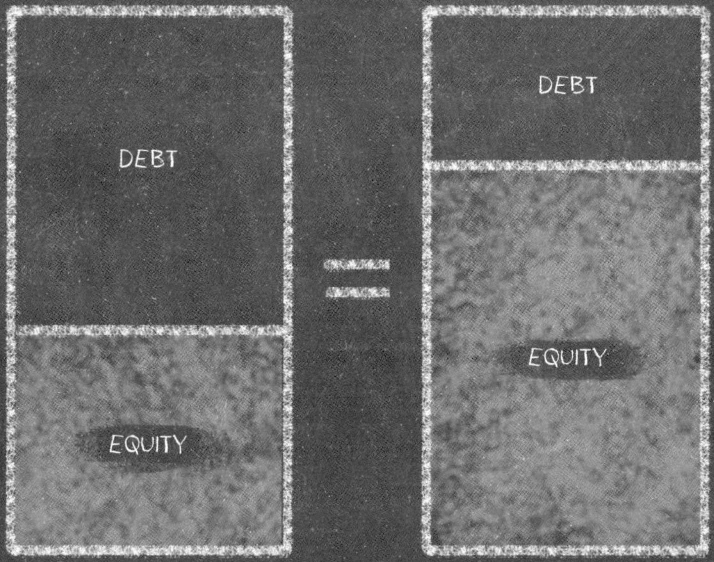
DEBT
EQUITY
DEBT
EQUITY

Forecasting

Economic forecasters build mathematical models of the economy. The models are made up of many equations, each describing a part of the economy: for instance, there might be an equation showing the link between movements in interest rates and investment by firms. Together, the equations can then be used to forecast future economic trends from the current state of the economy.

Forecasts are important to the financial markets, whose participants use them as a guide to investment strategy. An important element of forecasting is the use of leading indicators – variables that tend to herald broader changes in the economy. For example, movements in the stock market often anticipate the direction of the overall economy. However, forecasting is fraught with difficulty – the economy is so complex that it is hard to build a watertight and comprehensive model – simplifying assumptions need to be made, and forecasts frequently err.

The existence of firms

In recent years there has been a trend for firms to contract out many of their functions. The testing of products might be contracted to an independent laboratory, where it used to be carried out within the firm. What if this continued until *all* functions were contracted out – why would the firm need to exist at all? Economists have tried to answer this question using the notion of 'transaction costs'.

The purchase of an apple is simple: parties to the transaction don't need to gather complex information or take account of many uncertainties, so transaction costs are low. But many other economic relationships continue over time, are far more complex and take place in environments of uncertainty – they may involve high transaction costs. Employees of firms carry out complex tasks that can change over time in unanticipated ways: it might be impossible to specify all of these explicitly in a contract to a third party, so it may be more efficient for certain parts of production to remain organized as firms.

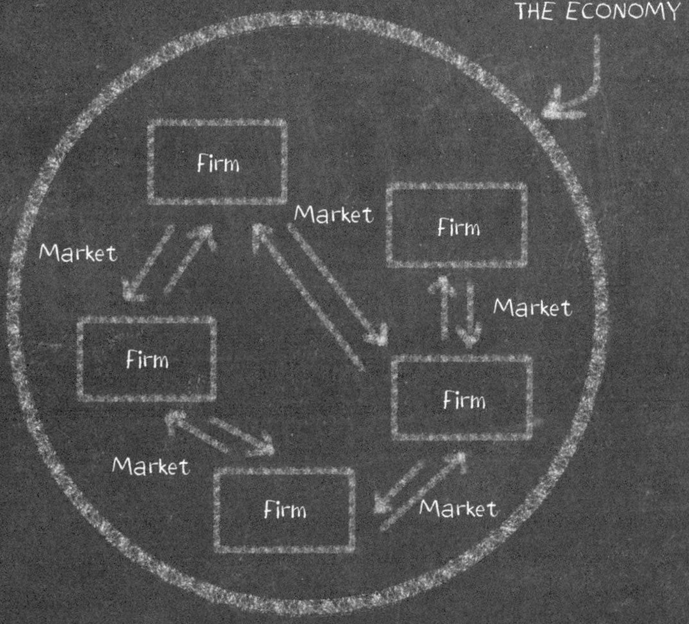
THE ECONOMY
Firm
Market
Firm
Market
Firm
Market
Firm
Market
Firm
Market

Profit maximization

Economists view firms as profit maximizers. Their decisions about how much to produce, how many workers to hire and where to buy their raw materials are all aimed at maximizing profit – the difference between total revenues and total costs. This may seem obvious, but it is not the only objective that might influence a firm. For example, a manager might aim at expanding the size of the firm so as to boost revenues, but this might not maximize profits if overall costs rose significantly.

When firms set output to maximize profits they make 'marginal' calculations: they compare the extra revenue and extra cost from one more unit of output. Suppose the 'marginal revenue' for a clothes firm from producing an extra shirt is £10, while the 'marginal cost' is £7. The firm will produce this extra shirt because it adds more to revenue than to costs, increasing profit. The firm will keep producing until the marginal revenue from an extra shirt is equal to the marginal cost of producing it – a production level at which profits are maximized.

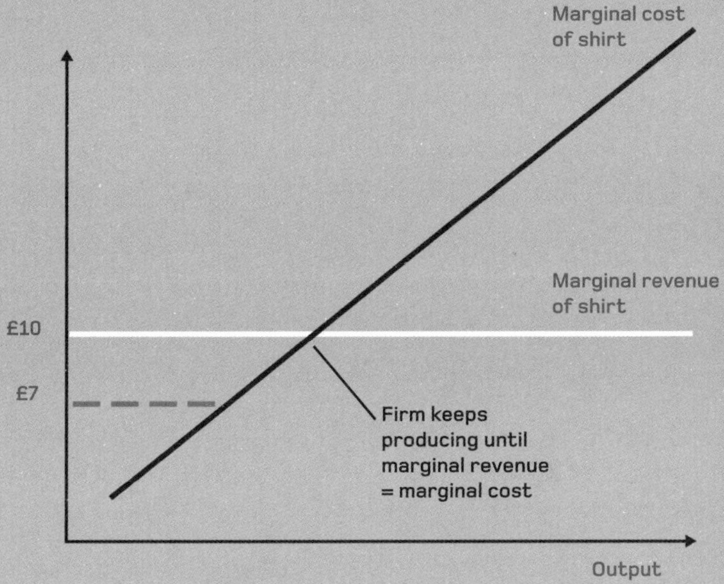
Marginal cost
of shirt
Marginal revenue
of shirt
£10
£7
Firm keeps
producing until
marginal revenue
= marginal cost
Output

Ownership and control of firms

The recent controversies over corporate bonuses and executive pay connect with a broader debate about how firms are managed. With the rise of the modern corporation, ownership and management of firms has become separated: companies are owned by their shareholders, but they are run by professional managers, and the interests of shareholders and managers do not necessarily coincide. Shareholders want high profits as this increases their wealth, while salaried managers might be less concerned with the profit of the firm as a whole than with their pay and perks.

In this case, the question is how best can shareholders monitor managers and get them to act to raise the value of the firm? This is far from straightforward, particularly when a firm is owned by a large number of small shareholders with little detailed knowledge of its day-to-day operations. With so many shareholders it can be hard for them to organize and respond to the actions of management when things go wrong.

Динамика показателей СМАД
после курса ДЭНС-терапии

Public companies and limited liability

A public company or corporation is one that issues shares that can be freely traded on the stock market, and benefits from what is known as limited liability. If such a company goes bankrupt, its creditors will seek to recover what they are owed by the company, but the individual owners of the firm cannot be held personally liable for the losses: they may well lose whatever they invested in the company, but creditors have no claim on their personal wealth. This is possible because, in law, corporations are treated as 'legal persons', with rights and obligations distinct from their shareholders.

Suppose you held a few shares in the bankrupt company, but had little knowledge of how it was being run. Limited liability enshrines the principle that you shouldn't lose your house because of mistakes that may have been made that led to the company's demise. This lowers the risks of making investments in firms about which one may have little knowledge, and so helps expand financing opportunities for companies.

Production functions

Economics has surprisingly little to say about the operation of firms: it considers them merely as entities that convert a set of inputs – capital, labour and skills – into output. The production function is a mathematical representation of this: it might indicate that if a textile factory had 10 looms and 10 workers it would produce 100 metres of cloth per day. It also tells you what happens when inputs change. For instance in this example inputs have to be deployed in fixed proportions: one worker to one loom. If the factory installs an extra loom, it will only increase output if it hires another worker to operate it.

Other kinds of production allow a choice between capital and labour: a farmer might choose to produce 10 tonnes of grain using tractors and a couple of drivers, or hiring many labourers to work by hand. The production function also describes what happens to output when inputs are scaled up. If inputs double and output more than doubles – perhaps because scale allows specialization – the firm has 'increasing returns to scale'.

The law of diminishing returns

The law of diminishing returns states that the effect on output of additions of labour or capital falls as one increases these inputs. Consider a farmer employing a single worker on his field. The overworked labourer produces 50 cabbages a season. By adding an extra worker, the farmer may get 150 cabbages from the field. He keeps adding workers until eventually he has 30 workers producing 2,000 cabbages at every harvest.

What would be the effect on output of adding an extra worker to this workforce? Output may well increase, but by much less that the extra 100 cabbages that came from increasing the workforce from one to two workers. By the time there are 30 workers there is so much labour working on the land that the impact of an extra worker is small. There might even be a point at which there are so many workers that they get in the way of each other, so that hiring an extra worker actually reduces output. Hence, the old saying 'too many cooks spoil the broth'.

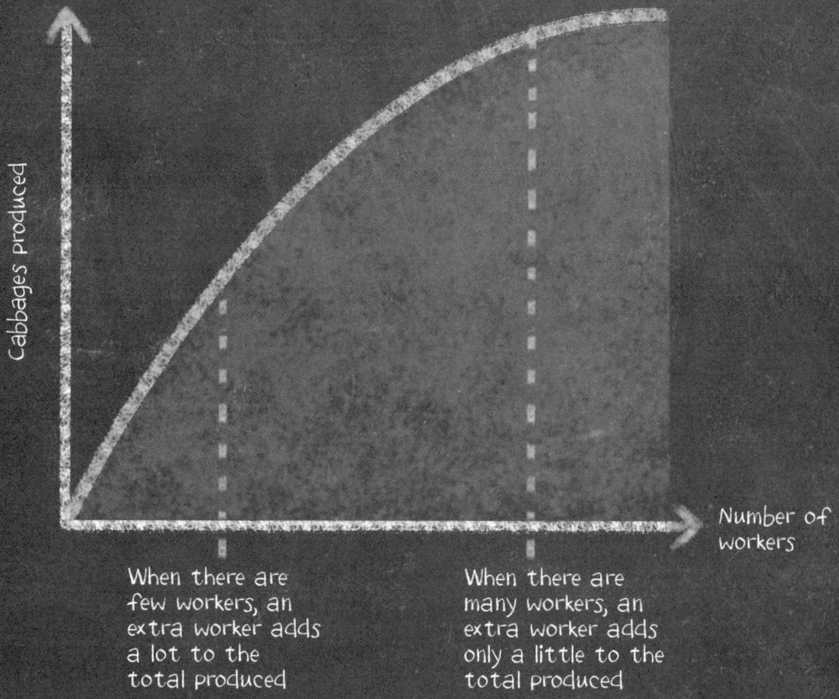
Cabbages produced
Number of workers
When there are few workers, an extra worker adds a lot to the total produced
When there are many workers, an extra worker adds only a little to the total produced

Average versus marginal cost

An important distinction in economics is that between average and marginal amounts – for example, average versus marginal cost. Suppose that a furniture manufacturer makes 100 tables at a total cost of £1,000. The average cost of manufacture is then £10. However, the cost incurred from making an additional table is not necessarily £10. If it is more than £10, then production of the extra table will push up the average cost; if less, it will pull it down. This is analogous to the scoring average of a football player – if in his next game he scores more goals than his average, his average score will rise.

Often the marginal cost of production rises with output because it becomes harder to squeeze out extra output when one is already producing a large amount. In making a decision about whether to produce an extra table, the firm must consider marginal rather than average cost: if marginal cost is less than marginal revenue, then it is profitable to produce an extra table.

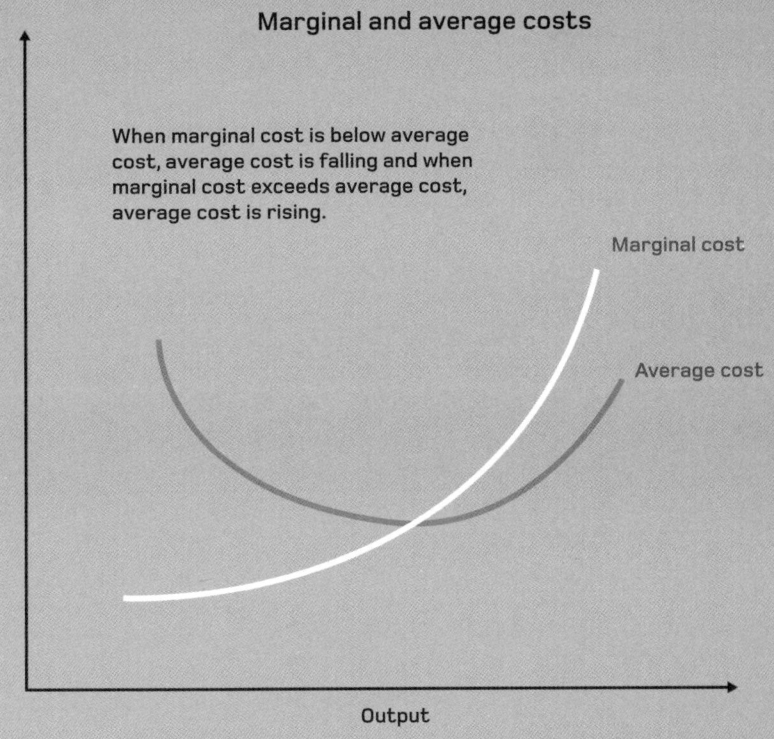
Marginal and average costs
When marginal cost is below average cost, average cost is falling and when marginal cost exceeds average cost, average cost is rising.
Marginal cost
Average cost
Output

Economies of scale

As a car firm produces more cars, the average cost of production per car varies. Increasing production from low levels, the average cost per unit will fall – a phenomenon known as economies of scale. Why should this be the case? Car production is highly capital intensive, requiring a large initial investment in factories and machines. As more cars are produced, these fixed costs get spread over greater output. In order to make use of its assembly lines, the firm also needs workers specialized in particular tasks – this improves efficiency and lowers average costs when production is high.

It is also possible for production costs to rise rather than fall as output increases. This might happen when the firm is producing so many cars that it is hard to coordinate different parts of the firm. Different departments may not know what the others are doing, perhaps leading to the duplication of efforts. Such a situation gives rise to so-called diseconomies of scale.

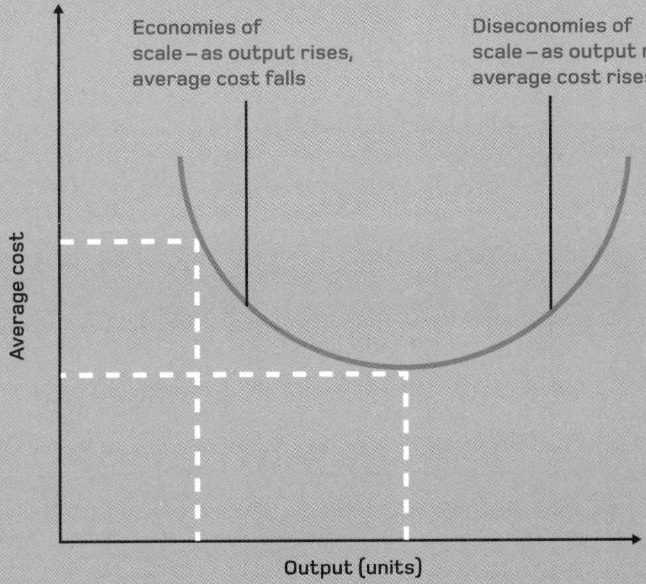
Economies of scale – as output rises, average cost falls
Diseconomies of scale – as output rises, average cost rises
Average cost
Output (units)

Sunk costs

In any economic situation, many costs can be considered 'sunk': once they have been incurred, they cannot be recovered. Suppose Dave buys a ticket to a play. On arriving at the theatre he realizes that the performance is *Macbeth* – not one of his favourite plays. It is too late to get a refund, but as he's spent £20 on the ticket, he decides to watch the play anyway. However, Dave's £20 is a sunk cost: he'll have incurred it whether or not he watches the play, so he should really write it off and decide what he'd prefer to do now – even if that is going home to watch television.

Similarly, sunk costs shouldn't affect how much a firm supplies today. A swimming pool owner has incurred sunk costs – the cost of land, the construction of the pool and so on. On cold days there may be only a handful of swimmers, but it might still be worthwhile to keep the pool open because the major costs are sunk and the owner might still make some money from the small number of customers.

Division of labour

A single man producing a pin would have to master many steps: straightening the metal, sharpening the point, attaching the head and so on. As Adam Smith observed, he would probably not manage to make many pins in a day. However, if the work was divided up so that different workers specialized in particular tasks, then a division of labour would be created. One worker might straighten the metal, another would sharpen the point, still another attach the head. Each worker would become skilled in his own specialized task, and many more pins would be produced than by the same number of workers carrying out all of the steps themselves.

The division of labour is an important source of productivity improvement. Adam Smith argued that it is what drives the growth of economies as markets expand and firms specialize in particular goods. Today, the division of labour and the 'production line' approach extends globally, as producers outsource the manufacture of components to overseas firms.

Perfect competition

A perfectly competitive market is one with so many buyers and sellers that no one of them can influence the price. In this kind of market, everyone sells exactly the same good – perhaps a commodity like corn or salt. If I buy some corn, then because there are so many buyers my purchase is a drop in the ocean of overall sales and will not influence the price. If a seller raises her price, no one will buy from her, and if a buyer tries to pay less than market price, the seller will find another customer. Buyers and sellers are therefore 'price takers'.

Another important requirement for perfect competition is that any firm can enter the market and compete for business with existing firms – for example, there must be no legal restrictions or difficult technological requirements to prevent firms from entering. Economic theory says that perfectly competitive markets encourage efficient use of resources, but of course many markets fall far from this ideal, containing monopolies or significant entry barriers.

Monopolies

When there are many firms in a market they compete and keep prices low. Suppose that prices and profits were particularly high in some industry. This would attract new firms who would enter the market and compete prices down. A monopoly is the opposite case – one firm controlling an entire market.

A monopoly can arise when there are high barriers – perhaps technological or legal – to competitors entering. Because the monopoly controls the entire market it can set the price of the good or the quantity supplied. Economic theory says that monopolists restrict output relative to what would be produced in a competitive market, leading to higher prices and greater profits. Economists tend to be critical of monopolies because consumers lose out compared to the higher output that would emerge in a competitive market. This is one of the justifications for competition policy, which aims at restricting the formation of monopolies.

Natural monopolies

Some goods tend naturally to be supplied by monopolies – usually those which see lower average costs of production as output goes up. Distribution of electricity is an example of such a natural monopoly: setting up a distribution network – underground cables, pylons and so on – is very costly, and because of the high initial cost, the more electricity is distributed, the lower the average cost. This means that a single firm operating an electricity network is far more cost-effective that two competing firms each operating their own distribution networks.

Given economies of scale, competitors are unlikely to enter such a market of their own accord, and breaking up a natural monopoly into competing firms might not be efficient. However, the power of monopolies may allow them to raise prices, so governments have an important role to play in limiting prices, particularly for utility suppliers. As a result, most governments tend to regulate, rather than break up, natural monopolies.

Oligopolies

When there are many firms in a given market, competition keeps prices low, while under a monopoly, output tends to be lower and price higher. But what about the intermediate case of an 'oligopoly' involving a small number of firms? In the 'perfect competition' model, there are so many firms that no single one can affect the price – firms produce on the basis of market price and don't worry too much about their competitors. Oligopolistic firms, however, are in a situation of strategic interaction: each firm's actions affect the price and the profit earned by others. So in making decisions about prices or output, firms have to consider how their competitors will react.

French economist Antoine Cournot analysed the case of two rival firms interacting by choosing output given their best guess of their competitor's output. He showed that combined output would be higher than that in a monopoly, although lower than that in a perfectly competitive market. In other words, some competition is better then none.

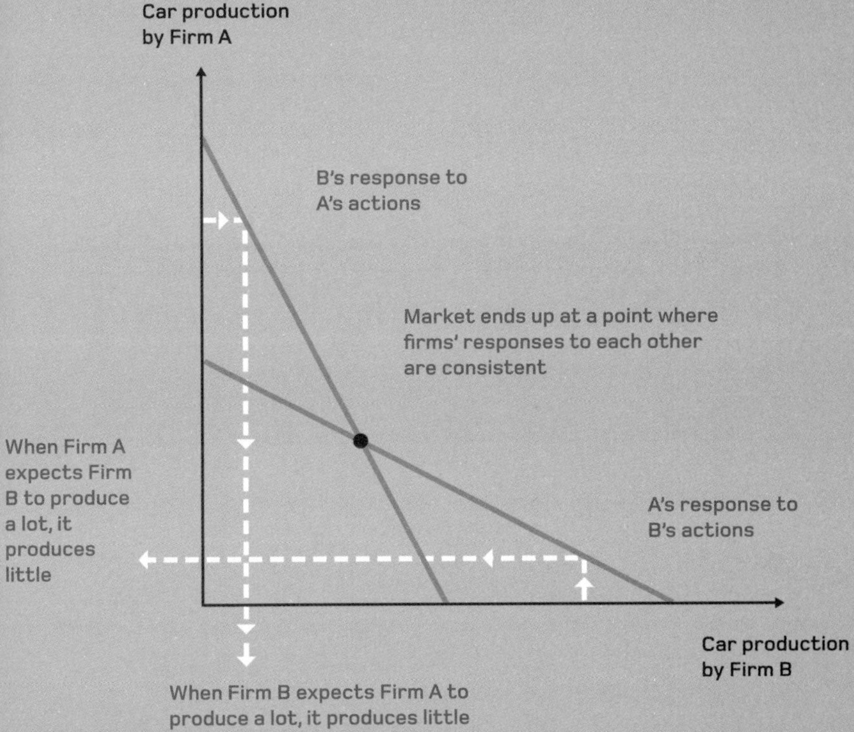
Car production
by Firm A
B's response to
A's actions
Market ends up at a point where
firms' responses to each other
are consistent
When Firm A
expects Firm
B to produce
a lot, it
produces
little
A's response to
B's actions
Car production
by Firm B
When Firm B expects Firm A to
produce a lot, it produces little

Monopolistic competition

Many companies sell soap. Each brand is slightly different but competes with the others: this is the essence of monopolistic competition. A consumer typically favours a particular brand of soap and is willing to pay more for it. This gives the manufacturer of that brand some market power: the firm could raise the price of its soap slightly without losing all of its customers. However, such market power has clear limits. Although the brand has special features, it is in competition with other brands. If the company raised its prices too much, customers would switch to other brands of soap.

So monopolistic competition combines elements of monopoly and competition. These firms have some market power and so don't charge the low prices that emerge when many firms compete to sell an identical product. On the other hand, because they are in competition, they cannot charge the kinds of high prices that a monopoly would. Such markets also offer product diversity, which is valued by consumers.

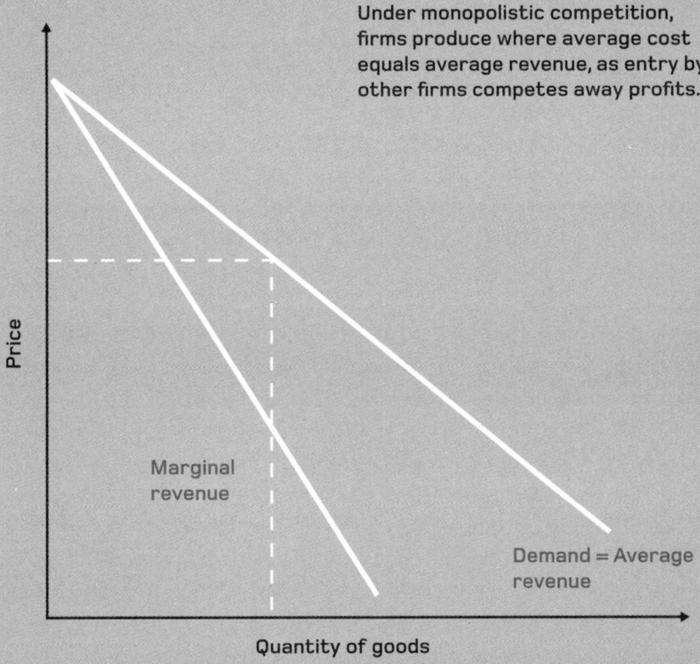
Under monopolistic competition, firms produce where average cost equals average revenue, as entry by other firms competes away profits.
Price
Marginal revenue
Demand = Average revenue
Quantity of goods

Cartels

In competitive markets, firms compete for business and offer low prices. Monopolies, conversely, produce less, charge more and make higher profits. So what if competing firms could club together and act like a monopolist? Such an arrangement is called a cartel. If members of the cartel restrict supply to keep prices high, all can make higher profits. In many countries such arrangements are illegal. However, some cartels take on an international dimension, such as the Organization of the Petroleum Exporting Countries (OPEC), a prominent cartel of oil-producing countries formed in the 1960s.

Cartels face a 'collective action' problem. Suppose OPEC countries boost the price of oil by restricting production. Now an *individual* oil producer, say Venezuela, has every incentive to produce a little more oil to sell at the higher price. If Venezuela faces this incentive, then so do the other countries, but if they all raise production, the price falls and they undercut their original aim. This is why cartels are prone to instability.

Price discrimination

A firm sells razors for $3 a pack, and its customers show considerable variation: those who value a close shave might be ready to shell out $4, while for others, $3 is the upper limit of what they are willing to pay. Is there a way for the firm to discriminate between these two kinds of consumers, in order to charge them different prices? If it could charge the particularly close-shaven men $4 and the rest $3 then it could boost its profits.

This sort of 'price discrimination' can be hard to do: even if the firm could distinguish between the groups, the less fastidious men could buy the $3 razors and sell them to the close-shaven men for $3.99. So successful price discrimination requires that different groups of consumers can be identified *and separated* so that one group can't just sell on the good. Student and pensioner reductions for haircuts are one example: concession status indicates that a person may be less willing to pay than average, but a service such as a haircut cannot be sold on.

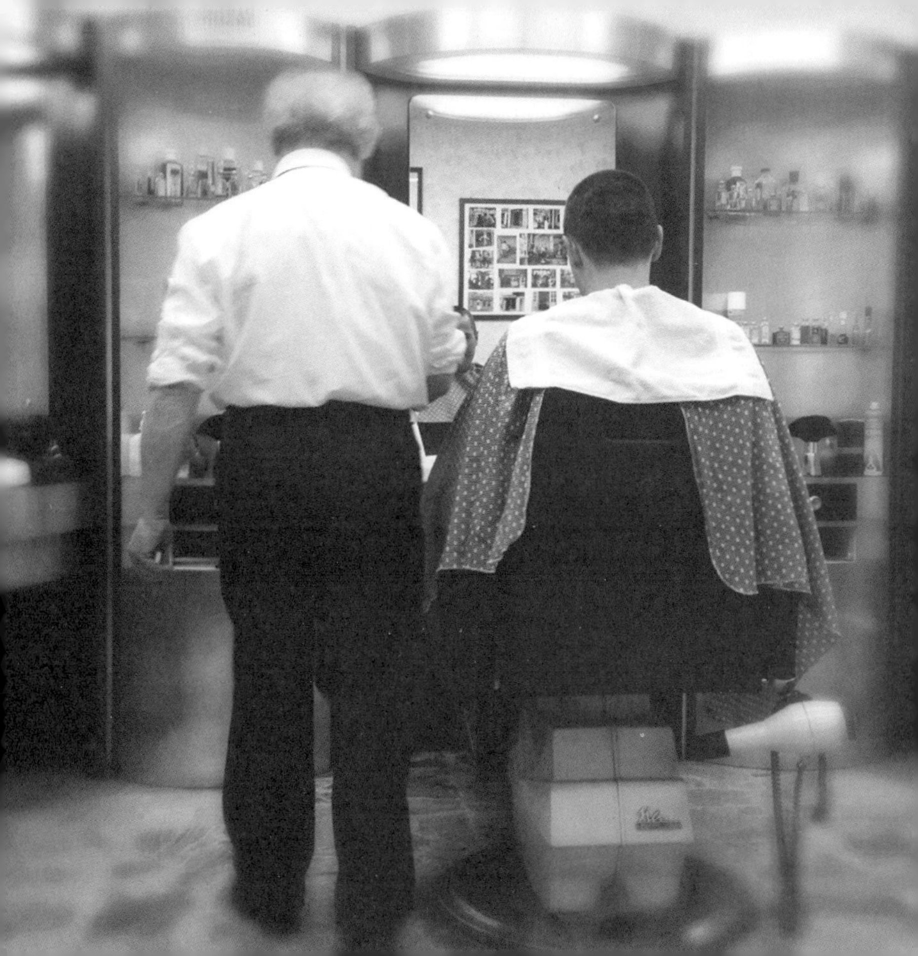

Predation

The market power of a monopolist is said to be undesirable because it leads to higher prices. But market power can also be exercised through price cuts. Some argue that such 'predatory pricing' is anti-competitive and that anti-trust agencies should try to prevent it. Suppose that Whizzy Bus is the only bus company on the London–Manchester route and earns hefty profits from its monopoly. Seeing an opportunity for profit, Zoom Routes now introduces a London–Manchester bus service. Whizzy responds by cutting prices, trying to drive Zoom out of the market. With healthy competition, fares would likely fall anyway, but Whizzy's strategy of predation goes further, slashing prices below the competitive level. In fact, Whizzy cuts prices below costs, hoping to recoup its losses from future monopoly profits. Whizzy calculates that Zoom would rather exit the market than bear the losses needed to compete. Distinguishing competition and predation is tricky. Moreover, it is unclear when predation is likely to be successful, since the predator itself may need to sustain huge losses.

Entry barriers and contestable markets

For a monopoly or a small number of dominant firms to sustain profits over time, there have to be barriers to new firms entering the market and competing with lower prices. Such barriers are often inherent to particular kinds of production. For example, entry to markets that need huge initial capital outlays and a large scale of production from the outset to pay for it may be hard. The production of some goods might need access to specialized technology that is not freely available, perhaps protected by a patent (see page 176). Sometimes existing firms have built up such brand loyalty and reputation that it is difficult for newcomers to compete.

Barriers to entry may also be legal: governments may confer exclusive rights on single firms to supply certain goods and services. When there are no barriers, firms can enter markets easily and compete. Sometimes the threat of entry alone may be enough to induce existing firms to charge more competitive prices: such markets are said to be contestable.

Patents

Patents grant exclusive rights over use of new technologies to their inventors. Economists normally think of such monopolistic situations as a bad thing because they lead to higher prices for consumers. The economic rationale for patents, however, arises from the fact that inventions have large 'spill-over' effects. Suppose that a firm invents a new kind of packaging to keep food fresher. Knowledge about this becomes available to other firms and they soon start to use similar packaging. The original invention creates benefits that spill over to other firms, and the benefit of the packaging to society as a whole is larger than the benefit accrued to the firm that invented it. The implication is that without encouragement, too few new inventions will be made relative to the high potential social gains. By making new inventions the property of their inventors, patents provide strong incentives for firms to invent new technologies. If competing firms want to use the technology immediately, they must pay the inventor, but after a certain period, the invention can be freely used.

Taxing corporations

The taxation of firms is often a vote winner for politicians – it seems fairer and less painful to impose heavy taxes on large, impersonal corporations than on individual wage earners struggling to support families. But this apparently persuasive idea depends on an assumption that might not always hold. Sometimes disparagingly called the 'flypaper theory of taxation', this is the idea that like a fly landing in the glue, the burden of taxes 'sticks' wherever it is imposed.

Formally, a corporation pays its own taxes, but who 'really' pays them? Consider a tax on an airline. This hits the firm's profits and it may respond by raising airfares, so consumers end up footing the bill. The tax reduces potential returns from investment, so the firm doesn't expand its fleet as much as it had planned. It offers fewer flights, leading to still higher airfares and the lay-off of some of its workers. This is just one demonstration of the way that taxes ripple around the economy and have all sorts of unintended consequences.

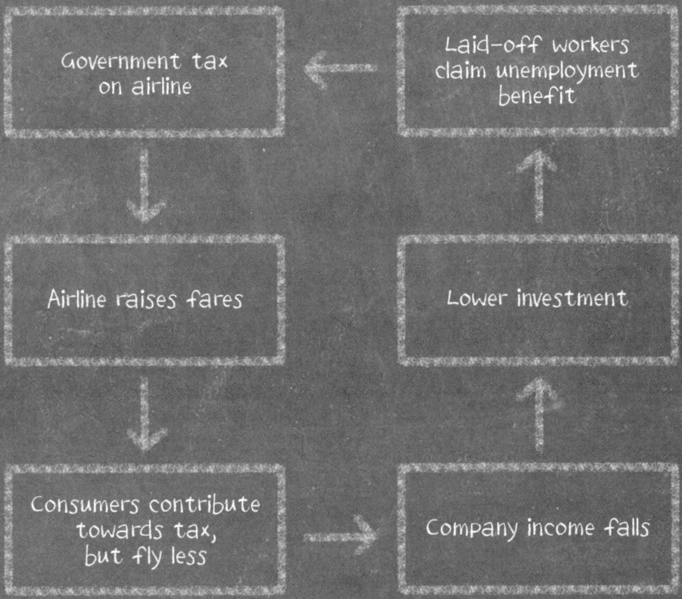
Government tax on airline
Airline raises fares
Consumers contribute towards tax, but fly less
Company income falls
Lower investment
Laid-off workers claim unemployment benefit

Advertising

Advertising is a pervasive feature of modern economies in which a huge variety of brands are offered to a large pool of consumers. What function does it serve? In much economic theory consumers are assumed to have all the information they need. In reality, however, they need to be informed about the prices of goods, their different features and even about where to buy them. Advertising provides this information. When consumers make informed decisions, markets work well: firms are subject to competition and prices are kept low.

Of course, a lot of modern advertising conveys little concrete information, but it can still inform consumers in an indirect way: when the quality of different brands is hard to ascertain, large advertising outlays can signal that a firm has confidence in its product. Advertising's many critics argue that all it does is generate new desires for the market to satisfy. What's more, enhancement of brand loyalty may actually hurt competition if consumers become less willing to switch between sellers.

WINNER!
2010 TONY AWARD
BEST MUSICAL
MEMPHIS
BEST NEW COMEDY
TV GUIDE
DON'T
BELIEVE THE
LIBERAL
MEDIA!
media research center
TOSHIBA
LED
LIGHTING
TOSHIBA
TDK
PITBULL
LG
2012
FRIDAYS

GDP and its components

Gross Domestic Product (GDP) is a key measure of a nation's income. It is the value of all goods and services produced in a country over a period of time. A country with a large overall GDP might still be considered poor if its population is very large, so an important measure of living standards is GDP per person (GDP divided by population). This provides a very rough indication of the amount of goods and services consumed by individuals.

GDP can be divided into different kinds of spending, such as consumption, investment and the purchase of goods and services by the government. Because every purchase involves a buyer paying a seller, it can also be broken down into the different incomes that get paid when businesses produce goods and services – these include wages and profits. As well as absolute and relative levels of GDP (between countries), economists are also concerned with the rate at which it grows, and hence how quickly living standards are rising.

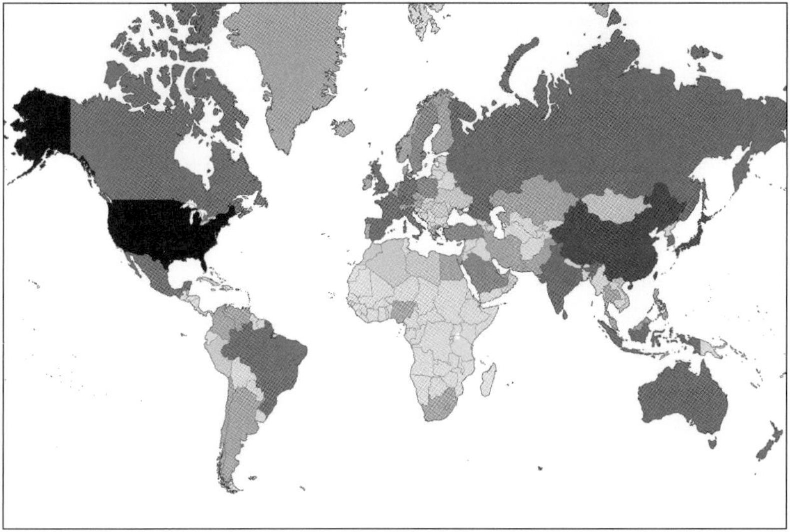

This map shows the nominal GDP of the world's nations in billions of US$.

10,000 plus
5,000 – 10,000
2,000 – 5,000
1,000 – 2,000
500 – 1,000
200 – 500
less than 200

Real versus nominal GDP

Suppose that a nation's Gross Domestic Product (GDP) rises by 10 per cent in one year. This might be because the output of goods and services in the country went up by 10 per cent. But it could also mean that the prices that we use to value the goods rose by 10 per cent while the actual output didn't rise at all. Often, growth in national income is the result of a combination of rising output and rising prices. Nominal GDP is expressed in money terms without adjustment for the impact of changing prices. Real GDP measures the actual goods and services produced.

If GDP rises by 10 per cent purely due to a rise in prices, then real GDP has stayed constant. In terms of actual goods and services available, the economy has got no richer. Economists calculate real GDP by computing the level of output at the prices of a particular fixed year. This removes the impact of price changes on the GDP number.

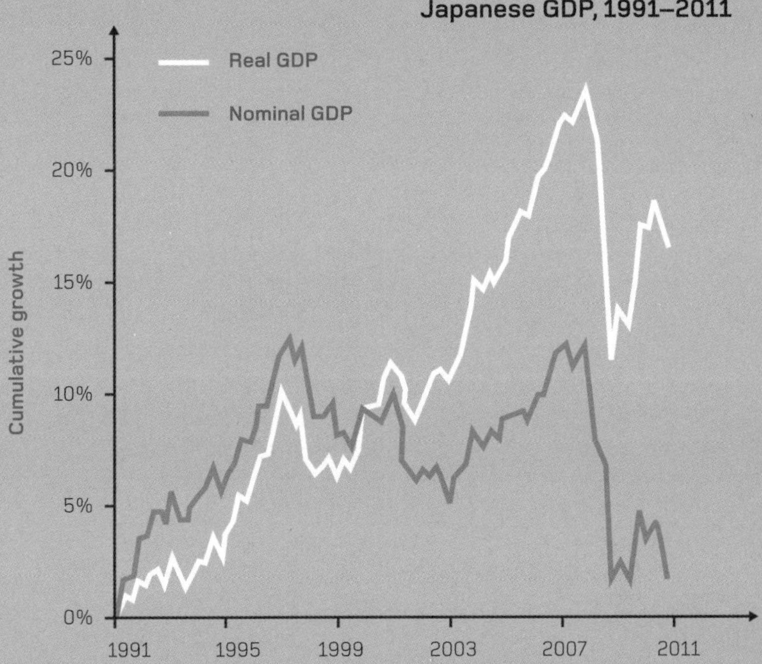

In Japan during the 1990s, prices increased faster than output, so nominal GDP outpaced real GDP. In the 2000s prices lagged behind output so real GDP growth was faster than nominal.

The circular flow of income

An economy can be thought of as a circular flow of income and spending between households and firms. Firms and households meet in two markets: that for goods and that for production inputs such as labour. In the goods market, money flows from households to firms as households make purchases. For example, when Pete spends 50p on bread, his payment for the bread becomes part of the bakery's revenues. In the market for inputs, money flows the other way as firms buy from households: the bakery needs labour, so it uses Pete's 50p to help pay its workers. In turn, the wage is used to buy another good and the circle is completed.

This way of thinking about the economy is fundamental to the calculation of national income. It shows that national income can be thought of in two ways: as the total output of goods or as the total income earned in an economy. The simple example given above just looked at wage incomes, but the circular flow also includes profits and rent.

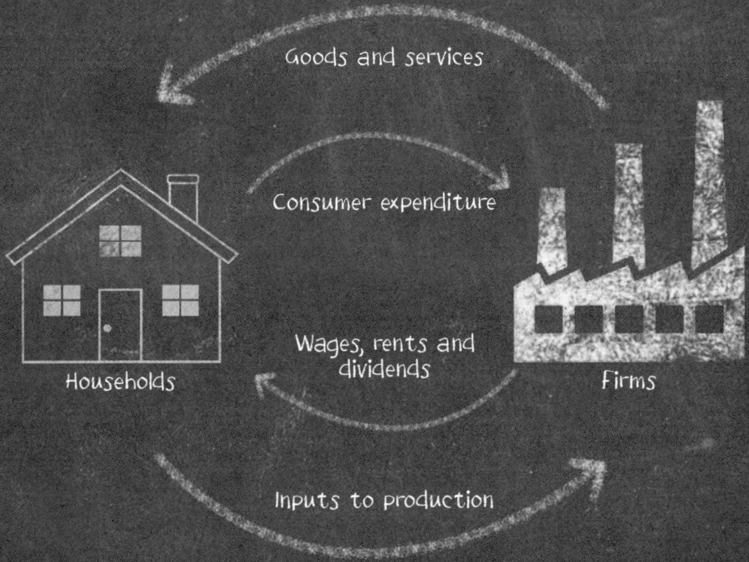
Goods and services
Consumer expenditure
Households
Firms
Wages, rents and dividends
Inputs to production

Investment

When economists discuss investment, they mean spending on capital that allows the economy to produce more goods in future. Capital includes machines and infrastructure, but also spending on the creation of skills through education and on knowledge through research and development. Investment is central to economic growth – only through greater productive capacity can the economy expand – but the amount of investment that is desirable is a more complex question than it might first appear. Investment fosters growth, but it can mean less consumption today.

Investment is affected by all sorts of variables. Because it usually involves borrowing from savers, the interest rate is an important factor. When rates are high, investors need to earn high returns from their investments to repay their loans and make a profit, so some projects become economically unviable. When interest rates are low, more projects are worthwhile and investment is stimulated.

Consumption

When you buy a shirt, get a haircut or eat a burger, you are consuming part of the output of the economy. Economists think about consumption at the level of individuals, studying how people choose what to buy given the prices of products and the income available to them. At the level of the overall economy, consumption takes up a major share of a country's national income.

Various explanations of the level of consumption have been put forward. British economist John Maynard Keynes said that when people receive extra income they consume a fraction of it and save the rest. If their income was zero, they would still consume some small amount, using savings or borrowing. Other theories look at how people decide between consumption today or in the future. When consumers take a forward-looking approach, higher income today doesn't necessarily translate into higher consumption: if they believe that the increase is temporary, they may save the extra income for a rainy day.

McDonald's
So CHIC
NetWork
YARGICI
C&A
Gloria Jean's

Government spending

Government spending makes up a large part of GDP in modern economies. Even in market economies like the US and UK, it is in the order of 40 per cent of national income. Historically, as economies have developed, governments have undertaken a wider range of tasks of increasing complexity. Provision of state education broadens, the government supplies more kinds of health services, and the welfare system provides for the unemployed, infirm and elderly.

Government spending on areas such as defence, hospitals, libraries and the education system all go into GDP. The other big category of government outlays encompasses welfare payments such as pensions and unemployment benefits: economists call such payments 'transfer payments'. Unlike the payment of a nurse's salary, for example, they are not made in exchange for any economic output. They merely transfer spending power from one set of people to another, and for this reason they are not included in GDP.

Aggregate demand and supply

Aggregate demand is the relationship between the price level and output demanded. Aggregate supply links the supply of output with price. Together they determine the output and price level in an economy. At low prices, aggregate demand is high as consumers' purchasing power is enhanced. Low prices also cut real interest rates, stimulating investment. Many economists believe that aggregate supply is unaffected by prices in the long run: this is because potential output depends on the actual capital, labour and technology available for making goods. In the short run, it is possible that higher prices might stimulate supply, but this can't be sustained.

The aggregate demand relationship can shift: an oil windfall might increase demand at every price level. In the short run, this may increase output, although in the long run because aggregate supply is unaffected the only impact is higher price levels. If supply is not influenced by prices, then the only way to achieve higher output in the long run is through investment.

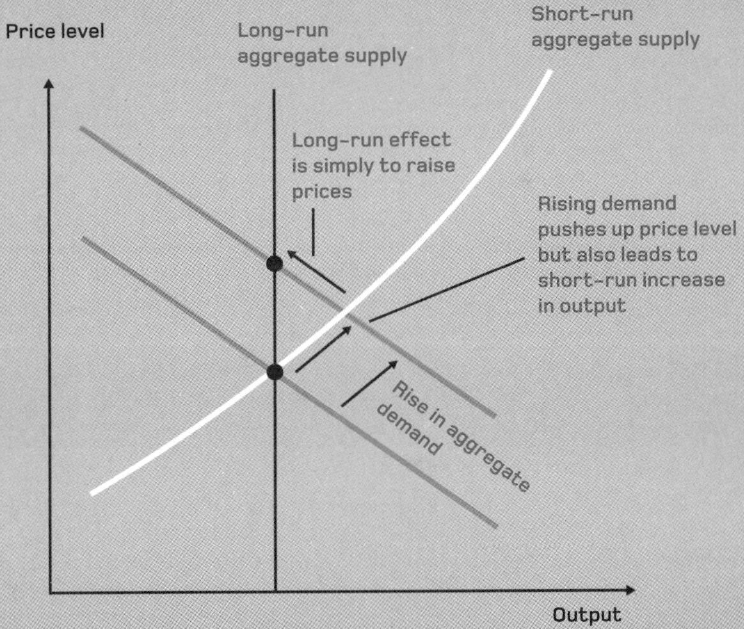

Higher aggregate demand may stimulate output in the short run, but may be felt later in higher prices.

Boom, bust and depression

Over several decades, an economy demonstrates a trend rate of growth, but from year to year growth fluctuates around this trend. In some years growth is below trend, in others it is above it. As a result, the economy naturally goes through sequences of booms and busts, known as an economic cycle. The more technical term for a bust is a recession, a period of falling output over a period of months or longer. Serious recessions, known as depressions, may last for years and see sharper falls in output and larger rises in unemployment.

Economic cycles can take on different shapes: sometimes reference is made to V-shaped cycles, featuring a sharp decline and recovery, and W-shaped cycles, when the economy declines and recovers, then falls back again in a so-called 'double-dip' recession. Much economic thinking has gone into explaining economic cycles and into devising policies that can help to moderate them – in particular, to avoid recessions.

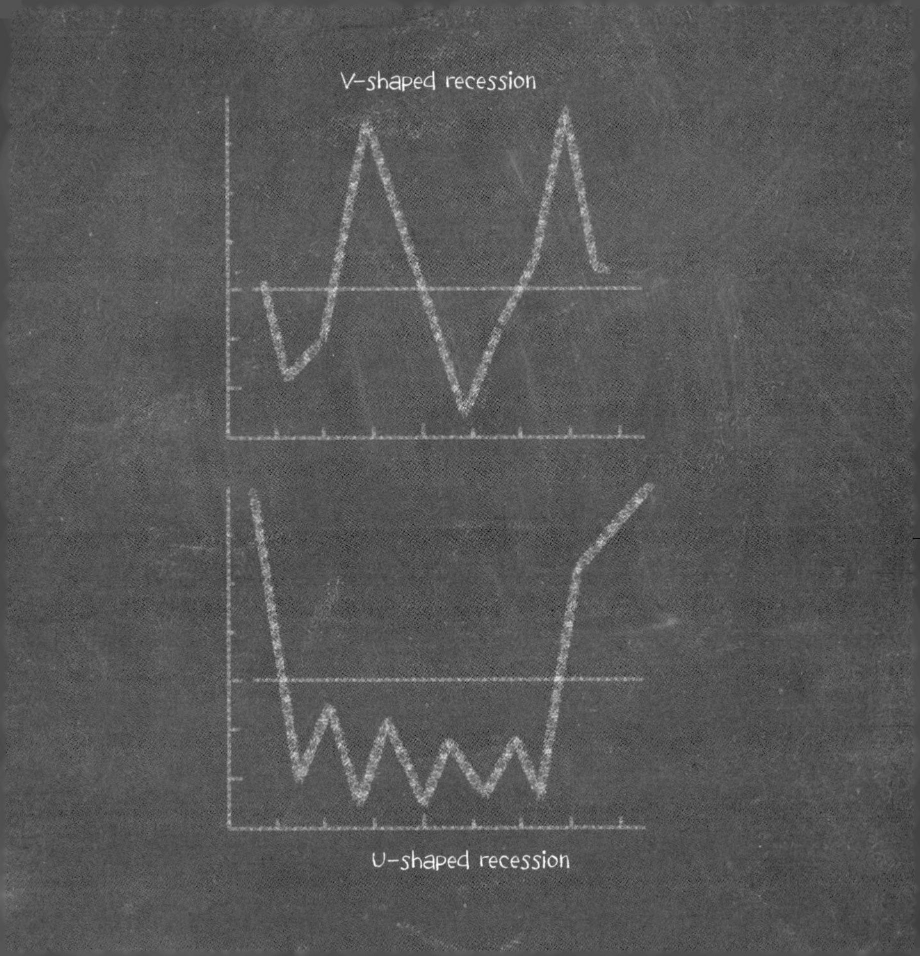
V-shaped recession
U-shaped recession

Unemployment and its costs

The unemployment rate is perhaps the economic variable that worries people the most, and it is probably the most politically sensitive. An obvious point is that unemployment causes great suffering: people who are out of work experience economic hardship and unhappiness. Sometimes unemployment is quite fleeting, as people move between jobs: it is people who are unemployed for long periods of time who suffer the most.

High unemployment also means that resources are lying idle. During recessions, machines and factories also tend to be underused because of weak demand, but unemployment usually gets the most attention. So when a high rate of unemployment persists over time, society loses out on goods and services that could have been produced if people had jobs. People who find themselves out of work for long periods of time can also get into a vicious cycle whereby their skills become obsolete and their morale is undermined, making it even harder to get back into work.

The natural rate of output

Often governments try to engineer short-term boosts in output and reduce unemployment, but many economists believe that economies have 'natural' levels of output and employment that apply over longer timescales. One idea associated with the concept is that governments can't push output and employment above the natural level for very long without generating inflation.

Anything that affects the ability of the economy to produce goods and services will cause the natural rate to change over time. Higher supplies of the basic inputs of production – labour and capital – will enhance economic capacity and cause it to rise. A greater stock of skills among workers will also do this. Over time, technological progress also has a huge impact on an economy's natural rate of output. Institutional features of markets can also influence the natural rate: one of the drivers of economic policy in the 1980s was the idea that reducing market regulation would make it easier for firms to produce.

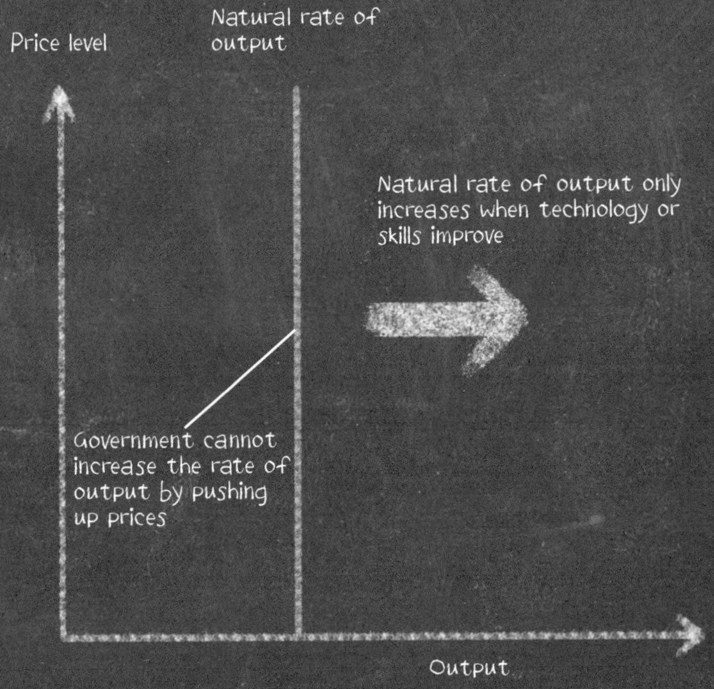
Price level
Natural rate of output
Natural rate of output only increases when technology or skills improve
Government cannot increase the rate of output by pushing up prices
Output

Frictional and structural unemployment

Unemployment has multiple causes. When economies go into recession large numbers of workers lose their jobs, but unemployment exists in healthy economies too, in a form called frictional unemployment that results from people switching jobs and careers. Because the labour market doesn't immediately match workers to jobs, it is said to have 'frictions'.

Economies are in a constant state of flux. Firms invent new products and stop selling others: when compact disks went on sale, tape cassettes rapidly became obsolete. Workers making cassettes were laid off, but in a growing economy they would be able to find new jobs in other sectors – perhaps working for compact disc manufacturers. However, the workers would still need some time to search for and secure new employment. The shift can sometimes take time, with workers in regions dominated by declining sectors often struggling to find new employment opportunities. Economists call this kind of more persistent unemployment structural unemployment.

Unemployment can persist when old industries close down, leaving workforces unsuited to new jobs.

The Phillips curve

In the 1950s, New Zealand-born economist Bill Phillips identified an inverse relationship between inflation and the rate of unemployment. When inflation was high, unemployment was low and when inflation was low, unemployment was high. The explanation for this relationship was that when the economy was booming and lots of people were in work, demand would be high, and this high demand for goods and services would push up price levels. Conversely, when unemployment was high and the economy was in a downturn, demand for goods would be weak and prices would fall.

Through much of the postwar period, economists took the Phillips curve to mean that there was a stable long-term trade-off between unemployment and inflation. By regulating economic activity through fiscal and monetary policy, it was believed that the government could effectively 'pick a point' on the Phillips curve, choosing a bit less unemployment and a bit more inflation, or vice versa.

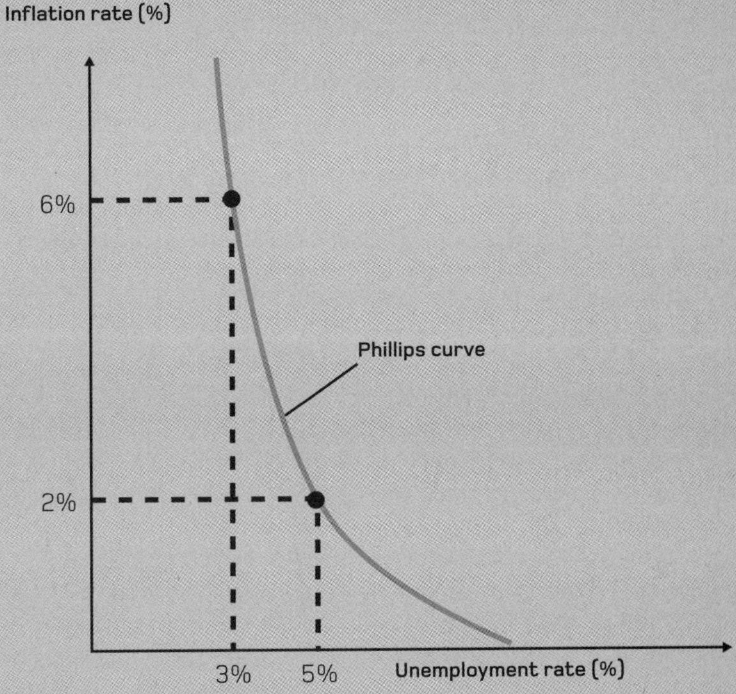
Inflation rate (%)
6%
2%
Phillips curve
3%
5%
Unemployment rate (%)

Stagflation

Stagflation was a term used to describe the twin ills of the 1970s: persistent inflation and unemployment. At the time, much economic thinking was based on the Phillips curve, which suggested that high inflation coincides with *low* unemployment (see page 204). During the 1970s, however, unemployment and inflation rose together, contradicting the Phillips curve.

New theories, notably those of Milton Friedman (see page 256), tried to explain this by denying that the Phillips curve really held in the long run. Economists had believed that by spending more money the government could boost the economy, driving down unemployment and pushing up inflation. Friedman argued that higher inflation would lead workers to realize their real wages were lower and make them less willing to work. Labour supply would fall and the economy would return to the previous level of unemployment, now at a higher rate of inflation. According to this view, the only way to sustain the lower level of unemployment was through ever-higher inflation.

In a situation of stagflation, unemployment and inflation rise together, as seen in the Australian economy during the 1970s.

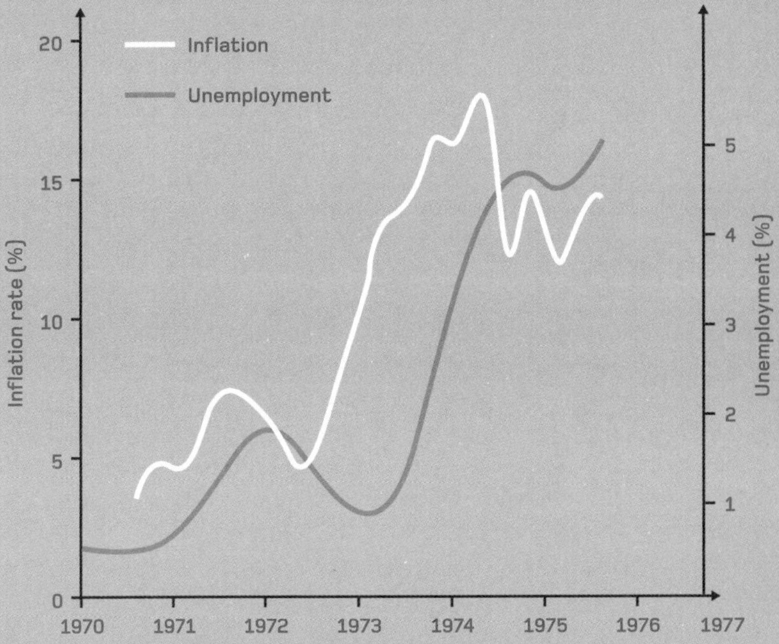

Hysteresis

Economists often think in terms of a natural rate of unemployment (see page 200) – a rate that corresponds to an economy's long-run level of output given its capital, the state of its technology and so on. The economy fluctuates around this natural rate: during a recession the rate of unemployment temporarily drops below it, and later reverts to it. Here, the natural rate is stable and is not affected by today's actual level of unemployment.

In a situation of 'hysteresis', this is no longer the case: high current unemployment pushes up the long-run natural rate. Unemployment is then more than just a short-term problem of idle resources – workers who will later get redeployed when the upturn arrives – it is much more serious, because it damages the economy's underlying productive capacity. One way in which this might happen is that when workers are unemployed for a length of time, their skills and motivation can deteriorate so much that they become unemployable.

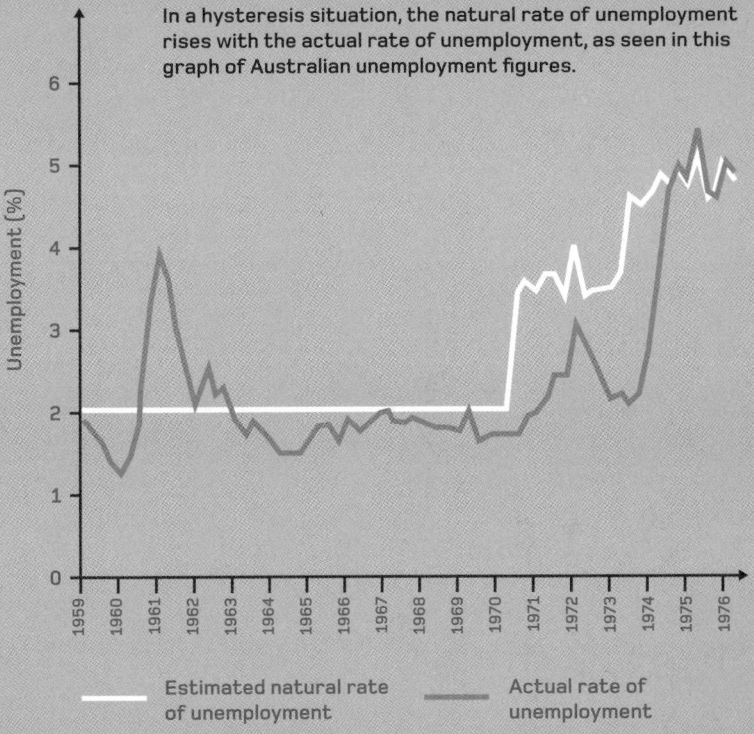
In a hysteresis situation, the natural rate of unemployment rises with the actual rate of unemployment, as seen in this graph of Australian unemployment figures.
Unemployment (%)
6
5
4
3
2
1
0
1959
1960
1961
1962
1963
1964
1965
1966
1967
1968
1969
1970
1971
1972
1973
1974
1975
1976
Estimated natural rate of unemployment
Actual rate of unemployment

Liquidity trap

Some economists believe that countries can become stuck in a liquidity trap in which monetary policies become ineffective. Normally, during downturns governments attempt to boost the economy by cutting interest rates to encourage investment. But if interest rates are already very low, it may not be possible to reduce them any further. In this case expansionary monetary policy (see page 248) will do nothing to help the economy recover: money is simply held onto as cash, rather than being lent out to fund investment.

An example of a possible liquidity trap was Japan in the 1990s, when interest rates were low and the economy stagnated. It has also been argued that during the economic troubles of the last few years many leading countries have become stuck in liquidity traps. One solution to such a trap is inflation: while nominal interest rates can't fall below zero, encouraging inflation can make real interest rates negative, which may help stimulate the economy by encouraging investment.

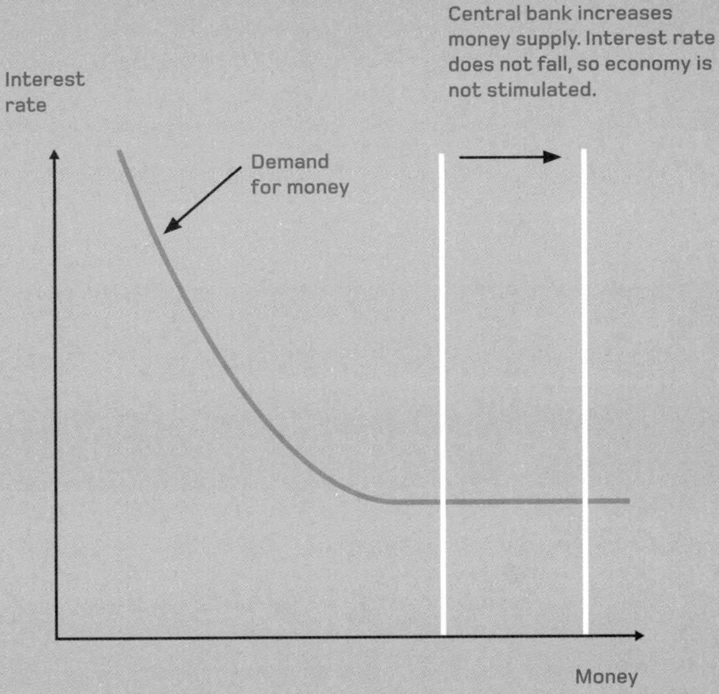
Central bank increases money supply. Interest rate does not fall, so economy is not stimulated.
Interest rate
Demand for money
Money

The costs and benefits of inflation

If all prices and incomes rise by 3 per cent then no one is made worse off, so why do people say that inflation is a bad thing? Inflation erodes the value of money, so one cost of inflation is that you tend to hold less cash and have to make more frequent trips to the bank. Firms also have to bear the costs of repricing their goods. If they do this at different times, the relative prices of goods change, and since markets work by responding to *relative* prices, inflation can distort them and upset efficiency. Another major cost is uncertainty: when inflation is high it also tends to be volatile, which makes investment planning much more difficult. All of these costs may be small when inflation is low and stable, but they can cripple an economy during hyperinflation (see page 220).

However, inflation can be a sign of a healthy, growing economy, and is often part of the process of recovery from recession. By reducing real interest rates and real wages it helps to stimulate investment and demand for labour by employers.

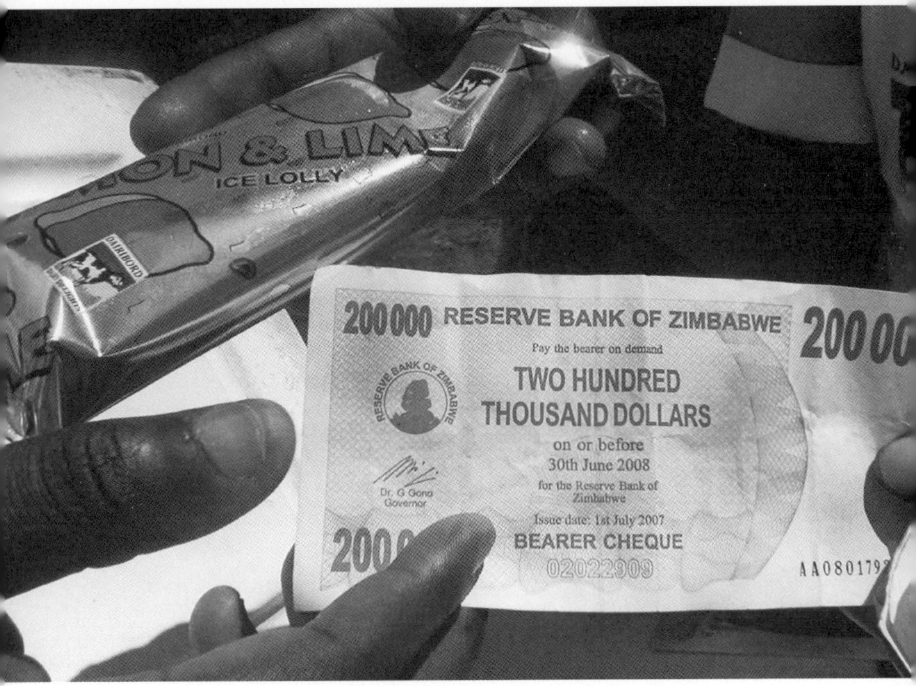

The inflation crisis that hit Zimbabwe around 2008 reached an estimated monthly peak of 80 billion per cent, and eventually forced an abandonment of the currency.

Demand-pull and cost-push inflation

The causes of inflation are often ascribed to the overall level of demand (demand-pull) or supply (cost-push). Consider an economy running at close to full capacity and suppose that the demand for goods rises. This extra demand could come from consumers, from the government wanting to spend more money or even from overseas residents demanding more of the country's exports. The economy could not, in the short run, produce many new goods, so the outcome would be too few goods being chased by too much cash, resulting in rising prices.

Another cause of inflation would be if the economy's supply capacity was hindered. This could happen if there were rises in the cost of firms' inputs of raw material and labour. Firms would be unable to maintain the same level of profit at current levels of production and would pass the cost increases on through increased prices. The inflation of the 1970s has been linked in part to the cost-push effects of oil price shocks.

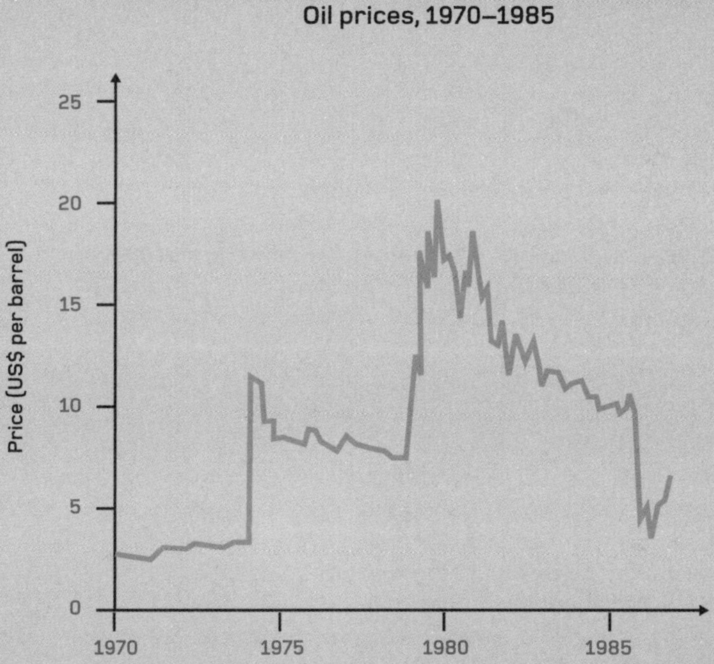
Oil prices, 1970–1985
Price (US$ per barrel)
25
20
15
10
5
0
1970
1975
1980
1985

The cost of living

When the cocoa harvest fails, the price of chocolate naturally rises. Aside from consumers who spend most of their money on chocolate, this will not affect the overall cost of living very much, and at the same time other prices may well be falling. The cost of living as a whole goes up when many of the goods bought by consumers rise at the same time – as during periods of inflation.

The consumer price index is a way of capturing this. It is calculated by first compiling the basket of goods – apples, shirts, electricity, bus tickets and so on – bought by a 'typical' consumer, and calculating its total cost. Changes in the cost of living can be tracked over time by comparing the cost of the basket in different years. One complexity in measuring the cost of living arises from the fact that the typical basket of goods changes over time: in 1850 the basket would have contained lamp oil and candles, by 1980, these would have been replaced by electricity and televisions sets.

1980

$10.00

2010

$33.00

The quantity theory of money

Imagine that one day everyone is given £10,000 in cash. People rush to the shops to spend their windfall, but the same number of goods are available as before. One outcome of the windfalls would surely be an increase in prices as so many people chase after limited supply. This is the basic intuition behind the quantity theory of money, which in its simplest form states that if the money supply doubles, then so will the price level.

One implication of this theory is that changes in the money supply have no effect on the real economy. In practice, the impact of money on the economy may be more complicated than the theory suggests: some argue that increases in the money supply can affect real economic output, particularly in the short run. Nevertheless, the theory is a useful way of thinking about the difference between real economic variables – those referring to actual goods and services – and nominal variables – those expressed in money terms.

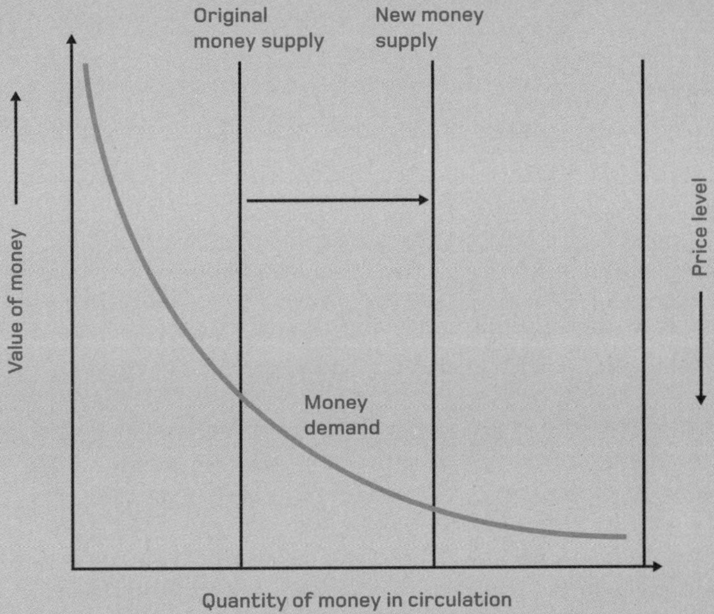

When prices are high people need a lot of money to pay for goods. When money supply rises, money is worth less and prices increase.

Hyperinflation

Hyperinflation has been defined as monthly inflation of above 50 per cent. At these levels, inflation can cause wholesale economic collapse. Episodes of hyperinflation are caused by governments printing huge amounts of money in order to meet spending needs. Often this happens when they are in dire financial straits – with a high budget deficit or debt level (see page 270) and little capacity to raise taxes or borrow. These were the conditions around German hyperinflation in the 1920s.

Even in normal economic times, the creation of money by governments is one source of revenue – as this creates inflation it can be thought of as an 'inflation tax'. Under hyperinflation, this process goes so far and so fast that the system of money breaks down. Because money loses value so fast, people spend it immediately, attempting to hold their wealth as goods or as foreign currency. Scenes of people going to the shops with wheelbarrows full of notes are emblematic of the economic disintegration caused by hyperinflation.

During its hyperinflation crisis in the early 1930s, Germany was forced to print banknotes with values of tens of millions of marks.

Rational expectations

In recent decades, economists have become interested in how buyers and sellers form expectations about the future. When making a decision about what kind of mortgage to take out, whether to go to college or where to locate a new factory, some view about the future direction of the economy needs to be taken. If one believes that interest rates are set to rise, then it makes sense to take out a fixed-rate mortgage now.

How do people form these expectations? They might use rough rules of thumb – for example, using this year's rate of inflation as a guide to next year's. The theory of 'rational expectations' says that they are much more sophisticated than this: people forecast the movement of economic variables using all available information and a correct model of the economy. If they didn't do this, they would make less than optimal decisions. The assumption of rational expectations has profound implications for the impact of government policies, but many question whether people are really able to forecast with such precision.

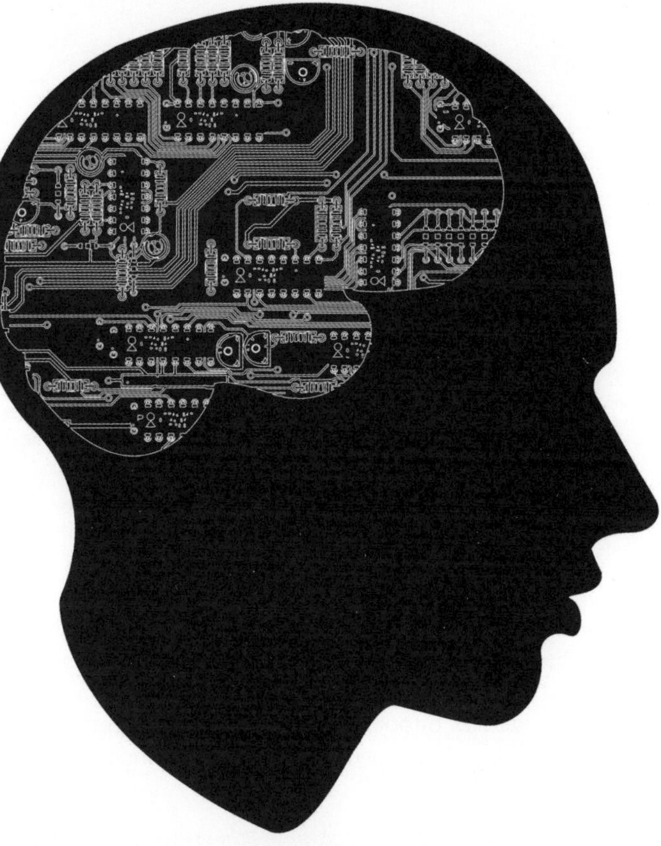

The life cycle and permanent income

If people are rational they ought to decide how much to save and how much to spend not according to their month-by-month income, but by considering financial flows across their entire lifespans. The life cycle hypothesis says that people try to keep their spending fairly constant over time, smoothing their consumption by borrowing and saving. When young, people save some of their income for when they are old. When they are old they use these savings to finance their consumption.

A related idea is that of permanent income: anticipated lifetime income that is related to a person's assets and skills. When an individual experiences a windfall, he realizes that this is a temporary rather than a permanent boost to income and so does not increase his spending, instead saving the extra transitory income. Similarly, people may borrow or use savings when their income falls temporarily. In this theory, the only thing that causes people to increase or decrease their consumption is when their permanent, long-run income changes.

Income and wealth over a typical lifetime

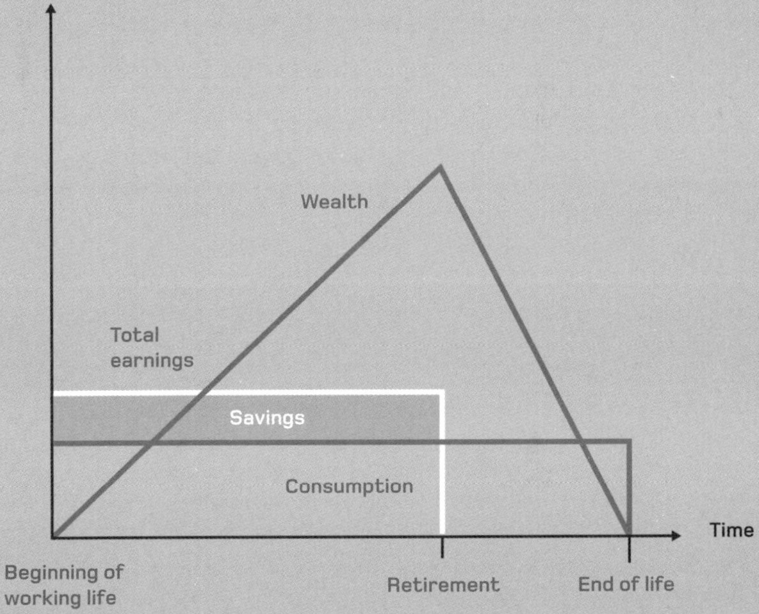

The Keynesian multiplier

Mary's aunt gives her £20 for her birthday, which she spends on new plants for her garden. The plant shop gains £20 and part of this revenue is used to pay the wages of the shop assistant. The shop assistant uses some of his wages to buy a sandwich, and some of the money that the café receives is used to buy tomatoes. As it diffuses through the economy, Mary's £20 gives rise to many other items of spending, demand for goods and services that go far beyond her initial purchase of plants. This is John Maynard Keynes's idea of the 'multiplier'.

Because individuals and firms generally only spend a proportion of their income, the impact of Mary's £20 eventually fizzles out. Before it does, though, it may have generated spending in the economy worth, say, £40. Keynes was particularly interested in ways that government spending could harness this multiplier: by spending money itself, the government might be able to trigger a chain of purchasing that would boost the economy by significantly more than its own outlay.

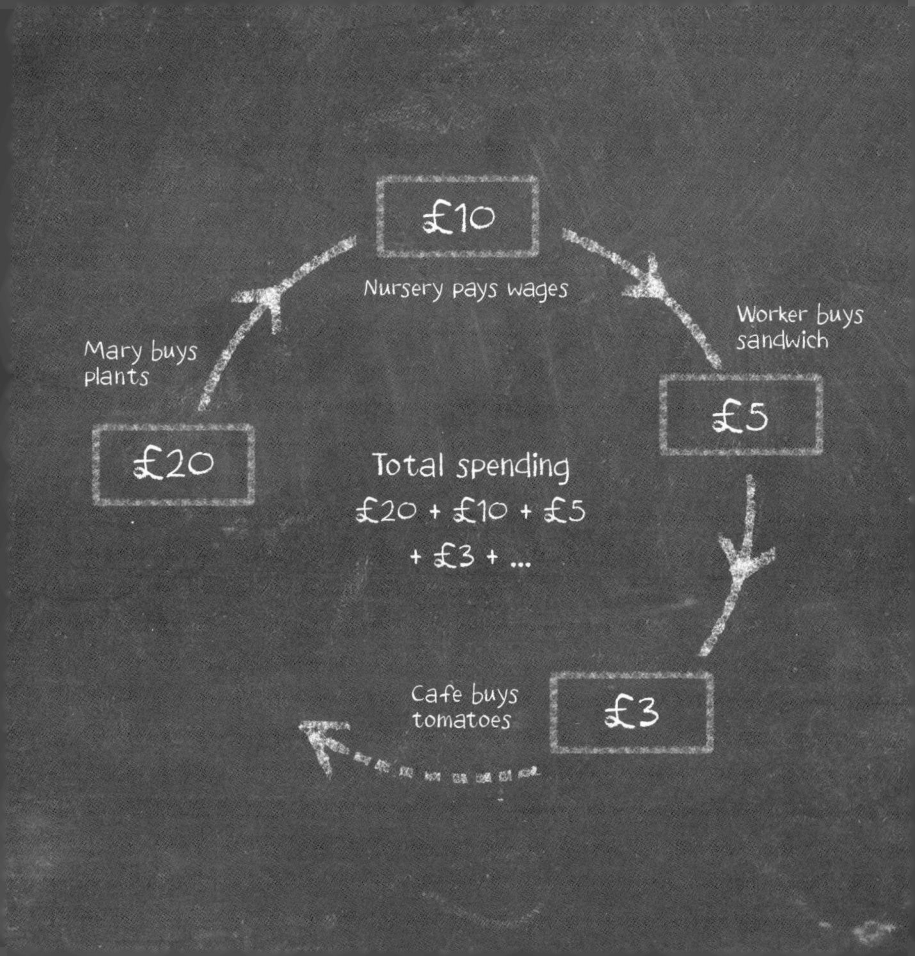
£10
Nursery pays wages
Worker buys sandwich
£5
£3
Cafe buys tomatoes
Mary buys plants
£20
Total spending
£20 + £10 + £5
+ £3 + ...

Automatic stabilizers

Governments sometimes try to smooth economic cycles by actively adjusting the amount they spend and tax. In addition, the structure of government spending and taxation creates 'automatic' stabilizers that moderate economic fluctuations even without active government intervention.

During a recession, economic activity declines. As incomes fall, the government takes less in tax: income tax, in particular, often falls quite rapidly because higher tax rates are levied at higher income levels, so as earned income falls, the average tax rate declines. As workers are laid off, the government pays out benefits, so spending rises. Tax rates and spending obligations together create an automatic shift towards more spending and less taxation that tends to boost the economy, moderating the recession. Conversely, during a recovery, the government takes more in tax as incomes rise. It also puts less money into the economy as it has to pay less in benefits. Now the automatic stabilizers work in the opposite direction.

The automatic stabiliizers of fiscal policy

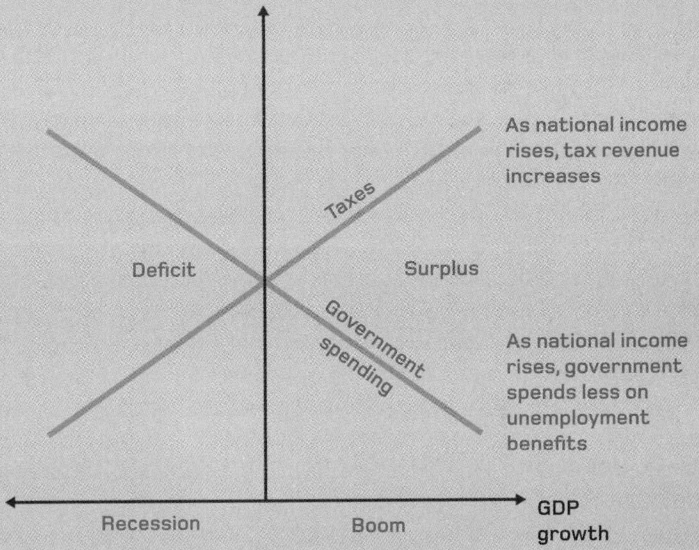

Real Business Cycle theory

Most economists blame booms and busts on imperfections in markets. The Keynesian explanation is that during downturns, wages are slow to adjust: the economy gets stuck below its potential output with persistent unemployment. But some economists have offered an explanation without invoking such frictions. The Real Business Cycle theory assumes that all markets function perfectly – prices adjust quickly to bring supply in line with demand – and firms and individuals are rational. As a result, the economy always runs at the long-run level of output permitted by available means of production. Cycles then arise because this long-run level changes. Suppose a new technology boosts productivity: output and employment rise in a boom caused by a 'real' feature of the economy. The theory, while ingenious, can be criticized: technology is a long-run phenomenon, so can it really explain economic cycles that ebb and flow every couple of years? Finally, while technological progress might drive booms, recessions certainly don't seem to be accompanied by technological reversals.

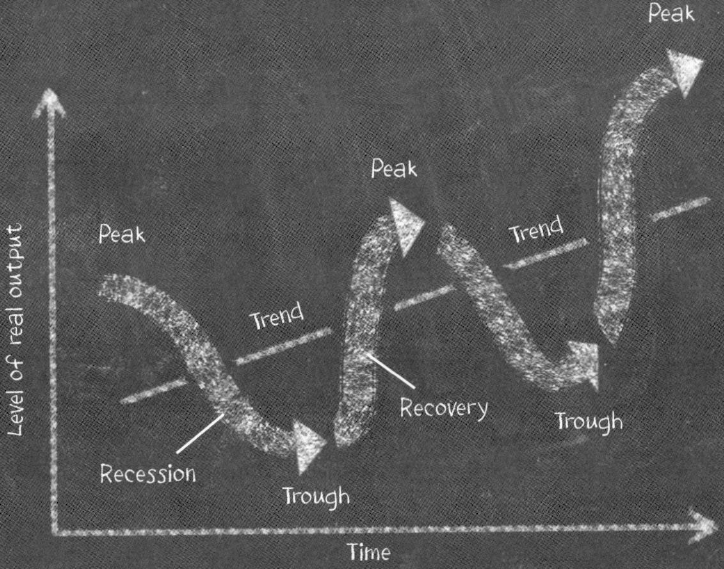

Although the performance of an economy can vary markedly over a cycle, average performance over the long-term usually follows a trend of fairly steady growth.

Money neutrality

People sometimes think of economics as the study of money and finance. In fact, its more fundamental aim is to analyse the production and allocation of 'real' goods: computers, pineapples, evening courses, heart operations and so on. Some economists – particularly those allied to the so-called classical school – think of money as little more than a veil over the real workings of the economy.

This leads to the idea of money neutrality – the notion that money itself has no effect on the real economy. If the money supply was doubled, the impact would be a doubling of prices; nothing would happen to production or the level of employment (see page 218). Money neutrality underpins the 'classical dichotomy', the separation between the real and the nominal (money) sides of the economy. In contrast, Keynesian theories show how money can affect the real side of the economy. Most economists accept that this can happen in the short run, and that it is really in the long run that money neutrality may hold.

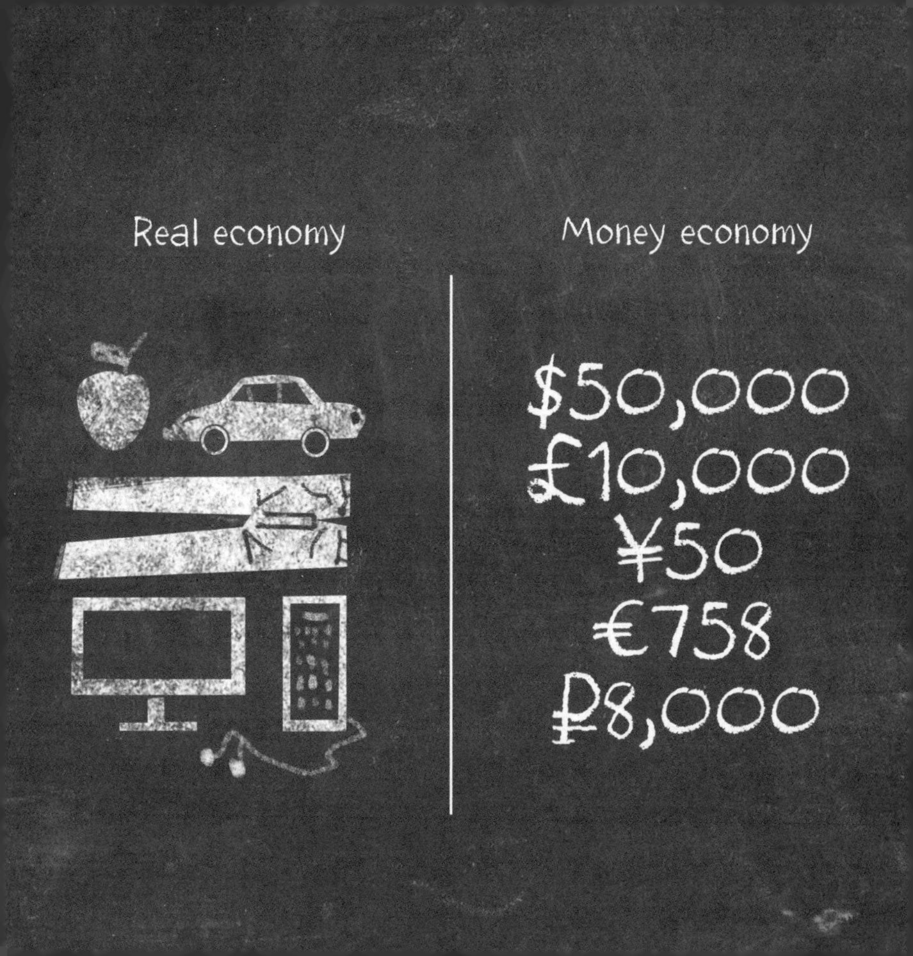
Real economy
Money economy
$50,000
£10,000
¥50
€758
₽8,000

The political business cycle

Some economic models tie the business cycle to political factors. In modern democracies, a government only stays in power if it pleases the electorate, so a struggling economy can cost a government the election. Governments, like firms and individuals, are rational and forward-looking: they will do anything that they can to maximize their chances of staying in power. In the run-up to an election, they have a strong incentive to boost the economy.

A government can do this by increasing spending, perhaps on hospitals, schools or infrastructure projects. It can lower taxes to increase people's spending power. It may also cut interest rates to encourage investment. These measures stimulate the economy, but can also store up problems for the future, such as inflation and too high a government budget deficit (see page 270). Once power has been secured, policy may go into reverse – hence, a government's political aims have the potential to generate economic cycles.

LG Chem
LG Chem

Demand for labour

Like the price of toffees, wages are determined by supply and demand. Firms demand labour, but this demand is a bit different to that for toffees because labour is not a final 'good' for consumption, it is an input to production. A restaurant employs chefs to produce meals that it sells for profit. The number of chefs employed is linked to the profitability of the meals. Each extra chef makes more meals, adding some amount to the restaurant's profits – the marginal product of labour.

But the marginal product falls as the number of chefs rises: when there are many, an extra one doesn't make as much of a difference as when there are a few. So how many chefs should the restaurant employ? If the wage is £30 and the marginal product £35, then it is still profitable to take on an extra chef. The restaurant maximizes its profits when the marginal product *equals* the wage rate. If the marginal product rises, the restaurant will demand more chefs: this may happen if meal prices increase or through some technological improvements.

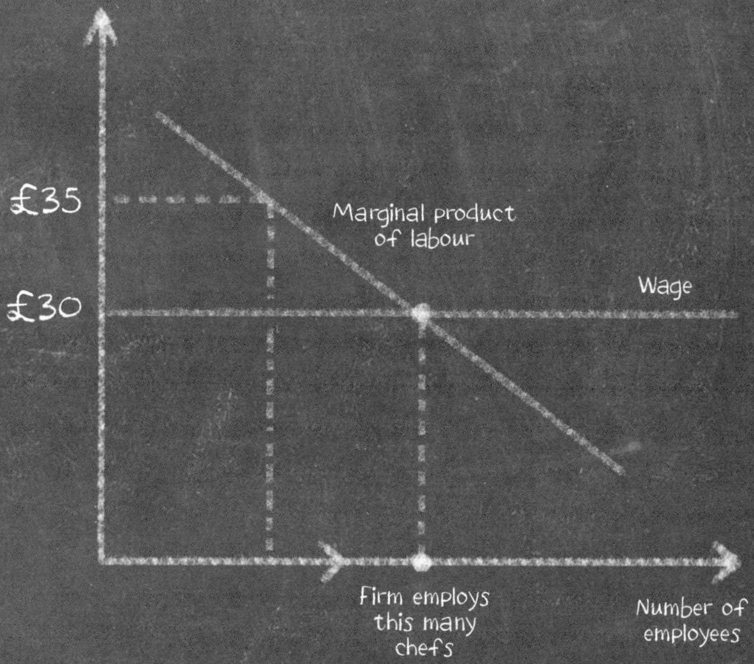
£35
Marginal product of labour
Wage
£30
Firm employs this many chefs
Number of employees

Efficiency wages

It is hard for an employer to constantly check up on all her employees and this gives ample opportunities for workers to shirk. Efficiency wage theory is based on the idea that an increase in wages can create incentives for workers not to shirk. As a result, it might be worth the firm paying more because of the increased productivity induced in its workers. The high wage will also increase the number of people seeking employment and so create a pool of unemployed people. The high wage together with the threat of unemployment if they are caught shirking, encourages workers to be diligent.

Another reason why a high wage might affect the efficiency of workers is that it allows them to eat well, a factor which may be especially important in developing countries. Efficiency wages may also account for the puzzle of why wage rates often don't fall during recessions – during a downturn, it may be more advantageous for firms to keep wages high and fire some workers, instead of cutting pay for all.

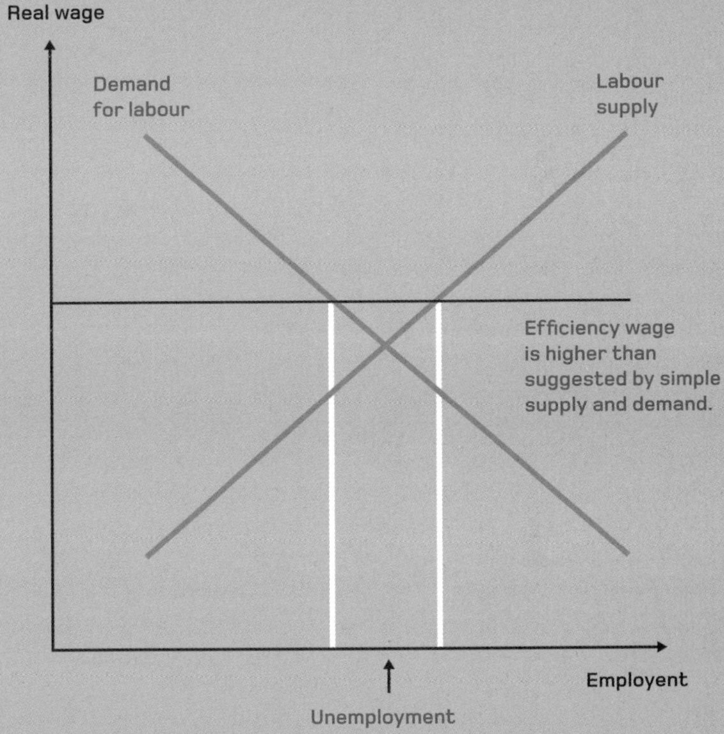
Real wage
Demand
for labour
Labour
supply
Efficiency wage
is higher than
suggested by simple
supply and demand.
Employent
Unemployment

Wage and price rigidity

Keynesian economics is based on the idea that wages and prices are 'sticky'. For example, when demand for labour falls, wages rates don't always adjust downwards. Even more, during recessions price levels fall so real wages actually increase. This reduces demand for labour from firms, causing unemployment. The 'New Keynesian' economists have tried to explain these wage and price rigidities. One reason is that changing prices has costs – the printing of new price lists and so on. Another explanation is that prices and wages are adjusted at fixed time intervals and these adjustments are not synchronized across firms. Consider that at the time a firm is reconsidering its prices, market conditions already point to an increase – but because their competitors will not be adjusting their prices until later, the firm holds off from doing this to stay competitive. The result is that price adjustment is sluggish. The message is that even when firms and individuals behave rationally, markets don't necessarily adjust smoothly, and so recessions and unemployment can emerge.

Wage rates often respond sluggishly to changing economic conditions, and in particular can be slow to adjust downward.

The housing market

Housing market trends are a weathervane of the economic cycle. During boom times, with the labour market buoyant, people feel more confident about the future and buy houses. With earnings growing, they believe they will be able to repay housing loans, and at the same time mortgage providers are keen to lend money – so house prices rise ever higher.

Conversely, when the economy falters, people lose confidence and housing demand falls, arresting the price rise. Problems in the housing market were at the root of the global economic crisis that began in 2007. In the United States in particular, economic growth and the housing boom were driven by a confidence that eventually turned out to be misplaced. Rising housing demand was met by ever more liberal lending – borrowers who could only afford to cover their interest payments were being offered loans on the expectation that house prices would continue to rise. When the bubble burst, the housing market became the mainspring of the crisis.

GDP and happiness

Gross Domestic Product is the most popular measure of a nation's economic fortunes (see page 182). But increasingly, experts are asking whether it is the best indicator of well-being. For one thing, the fruits of an economy are not always evenly distributed among the population, but a more fundamental question is how closely material wealth relates to well-being.

American economist Richard Easterlin looked at surveys of people's reported well-being and found that although there were correlations between income and happiness, the picture was complex. The richest countries weren't necessarily the happiest, and in some countries rising income did not equate to rising happiness. One explanation is the 'hedonic treadmill': people psychologically adapting to higher standards of living until they feel normal. Income is still an important determinant of well-being, but this new approach has prompted the invention of broader measures of well-being encompassing life expectancy, health and education as well as income.

In Bhutan, economic progress is measured in terms of national happiness rather than national income.

Stabilization policy

To maintain steady speed, a motorist takes her foot off the accelerator when going downhill and puts it back on when going uphill. Stabilization policy is based on an analogous view of the economy. When the economy enters recession the government can stop output and employment falling by pumping in money. During a boom, as the economy races ahead and generates inflation, the government can slow it by taking money out. Just like the steady driver, active stabilization policy can smooth the ups and downs of the economic cycle.

Stabilization can be done with fiscal policy (government spending and taxation) and monetary policy (interest rates and money supply). However, stabilization policy has been criticized: some doubt these policies are effective controls on economic output, and even if they are, the effects may come with a delay. Such lags, alongside the unreliability of economic forecasting, mean that by the time stabilization measures take effect, conditions may be very different from those planned for.

Monetary policy

Monetary policy is concerned with government control of the money supply: too little money hampers economic activity, while too much can stoke inflation. The government creates money by printing notes or by supplying deposits to banks who then lend out a proportion of these. Governments can also influence the money supply by setting a minimum proportion of deposits that the banks must keep as cash (see page 96). If this ratio is increased, then deposits create less lending and so less money.

The banks can increase their deposits – and hence the money they have available to lend out – by borrowing from the central bank, but when the central bank increases the interest rate it charges, the money supply is restricted. Finally, the government can extract money from the economy by selling bonds to the public – to increase money it buys back the bonds. Controlling money supply is difficult, since it can also be influenced by the behaviour of individuals and banks beyond government control.

Quantitative easing

The manipulation of interest rates forms a central plank of monetary policy: often during downturns, governments lower interest rates to invigorate the economy. But what if rates are already so low that they can't be cut further, as happened in some countries during the recent economic crisis? Quantitative easing (QE) is an alternative means of loosening monetary conditions by rapidly increasing the money supply.

The central bank effectively creates cash and, by purchasing financial assets such as government and corporate bonds, injects it into the economy. This lowers 'retail' interest rates faced by consumers and firms, boosting the economy. QE is a variation on a more traditional form of monetary policy known as 'open market operations', in which the central bank deals in short-term government bonds: with QE a broader range of assets are purchased. Since its primary aim is to bring down borrowing costs, QE should be distinguished from the printing of money merely to finance government spending.

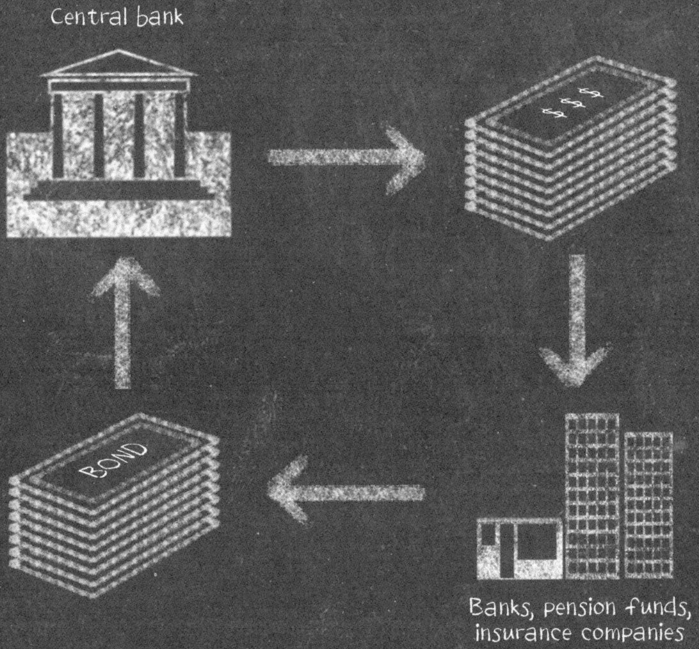

Central bank
$ $ $
BOND
Banks, pension funds, insurance companies

Fiscal policy

Fiscal policy concerns itself with government spending and taxation, and Keynesian economists in particular argue that it can be used to help pull economies out of recessions. If a government spends more or taxes less, aggregate demand rises, boosting output and lowering unemployment. By cutting taxes or raising spending, it harnesses a multiplier effect (see page 226) – a boost to demand that is larger than the spending rise or tax cut itself because the extra money gets spent many times over as it circulates around the economy.

Some economists are sceptical about the usefulness of fiscal policy. They doubt whether increased demand can really raise output, particularly in the long run. They also argue that higher demand as a result of government spending 'crowds out' private investment, because high demand pushes up interest rates and dampens investment. In the wake of the recent economic crisis, the debate about the effectiveness of fiscal policy has re-emerged with a new urgency.

British economist John Maynard Keynes advocated the use of fiscal policy as a tool for managing economic cycles.

Policy discretion versus rules

When Ulysses sailed towards the sirens, he ordered his men to tie him to the mast of his ship. Ulysses wanted to hear the sirens' song, but knew it was so intoxicating that if he was in control of the ship he would sail to their island and crash on the rocks. He knew the best outcome – keeping control of his ship and hearing the song at a safe distance – was impossible, so the best thing would be to relinquish control.

Some argue that economic policy faces the same sort of dilemma. Like Ulysses in control of his ship, full discretion over policy by government is self-defeating. The government promises to deliver low inflation one year, but the following year the temptation to pump up the economy to increase employment will be irresistible, resulting in higher inflation. Some recommend that the government 'ties itself to its mast' by committing to a fixed policy rule, come what may. One way of doing this is to hand over the levers of policy, for example, to an independent central bank.

Monetarism

Monetarism is a school of economic thought that stresses the importance of the money supply. Led by the American economist Milton Friedman (opposite), monetarists argued that in the short run there was a link between the money supply and economic output, but in the long run more money would simply lead to inflation. Attempts to fine-tune the economy through active monetary policy – boosting the money supply during downturns, for example – would be futile: even though there might be some short-run impacts, the lags between different variables would make it hard for the government to successfully harness the effects and in the long run the result would be higher inflation. Monetarism says that rather than fiddling with the money supply in response to the economic cycle, governments should set a fixed level of money growth and stick with it regardless of economic conditions. This was tried for a time in the 1980s, but it proved hard for governments to control the money supply quite so strictly.

Inflation targeting

During the 1980s, many countries' monetary policies were based on targets for growth of the money supply that proved difficult to hit. Since a key aim of the targets was to achieve a stable and appropriate rate of inflation, why not target inflation directly? US economist John Taylor proposed an inflation-targeting rule based on the adjustment of interest rates by the central bank in response to economic conditions.

Suppose the inflation target was 3 per cent. The rule would require a rise in the interest rate if actual inflation exceeded 3 per cent. This would cool the economy and bring inflation down towards its target rate. The rule also required a rise in interest rates when employment was above its long-run 'natural' level, and a decrease when it was below it. In recent decades many central banks adopted policies along the lines of the Taylor rule. Some economists argue that this fostered the relatively stable, low inflationary economic environment that lasted up until the economic crisis that began in 2007.

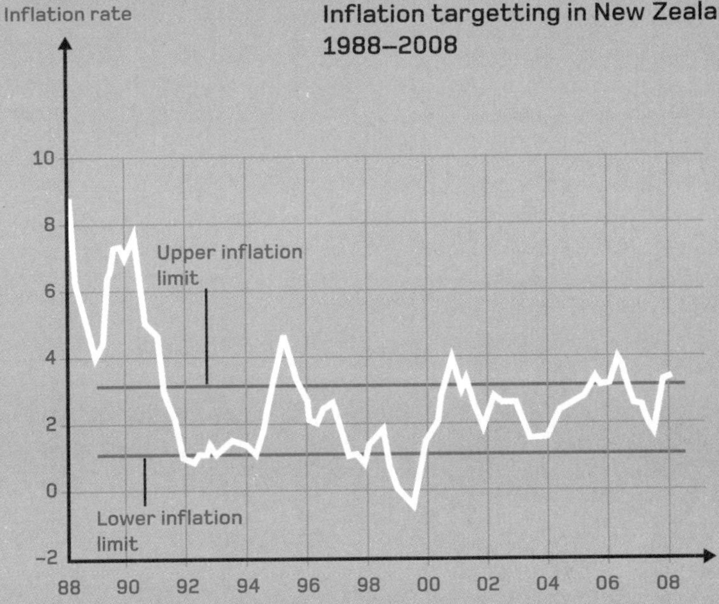

Targeting policies frequently aim to keep inflation between upper and lower limits.

The Lucas critique

In the 1970s, US economist Robert Lucas criticized standard economic policy in what came to be known as the Lucas critique. This formed part of a school of thought that introduced 'rational expectations' (see page 222) into economics. Lucas pointed out that policy is devised assuming stable relationships between variables – for example, that lower unemployment goes with higher inflation. He argued that the introduction of a policy would actually change the relationships forming the basis of the policy. This is because people, having rational expectations, would accurately anticipate the impact of the policy and change their behaviour accordingly, often undermining the original goal of the policy. For example, if the government tries to boost employment, people anticipate the higher inflation that results and realize this will reduce their real wages, discouraging them from working more. The critique, while fundamental, depends on rational expectations, an assumption that some call into question.

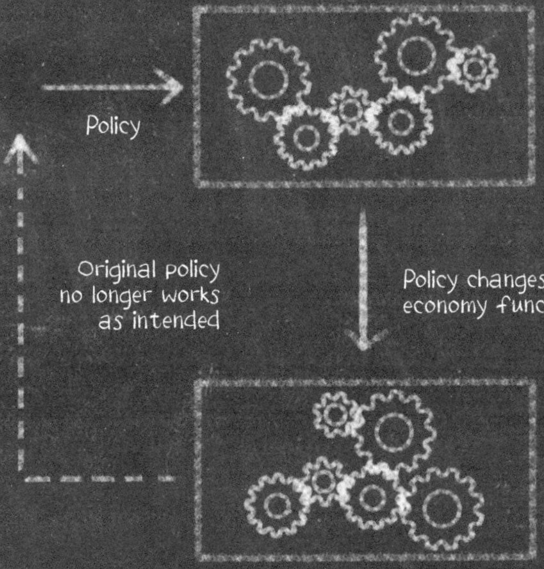
Policy
Original policy no longer works as intended
Policy changes how economy functions

Crowding out

One prescription for curing recession is for government to spend more: the hope is that this leads to a large enough boost in demand to stimulate growth. However, government spending can have knock-on effects that counteract the higher demand. The danger is that public spending can displace private spending if the former is a substitute for the latter. If so, then the increased demand caused by government spending might be partially or fully neutralized by a fall in some areas of private-sector spending. Even spending on defence and roads – public goods that can't easily be carried out privately (see page 58) – can lead to crowding out. The increase in aggregate demand causes interest rates to rise as more money is demanded by individuals and companies. Higher interest rates dampen private sector investment, so the initial boost to economic activity is offset. The issue for economists, then, is whether crowding out is a large enough effect to completely dissipate the impact of government spending.

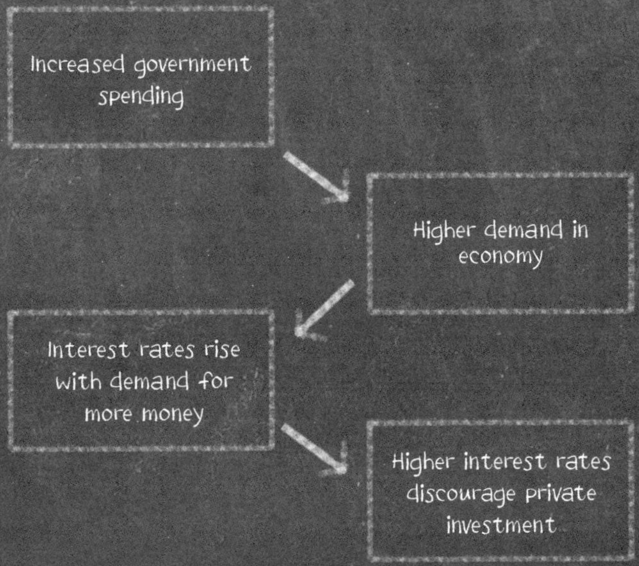
Increased government spending
Higher demand in economy
Interest rates rise with demand for more money
Higher interest rates discourage private investment

Supply side economics and the Laffer curve

During the 1980s, government policies to manage the level of demand in the economy fell out of favour. The focus shifted to enhancing the supply side of the economy – that is, to making firms and workers more productive. One idea was that high taxes blunted incentives and so hobbled the supply side – the implication was that cutting taxes would stimulate the economy. American economist Arthur Laffer proposed a relationship between the tax rate and government revenue that came to be known as the Laffer curve. One might expect a cut in tax rates to reduce government revenue, but in fact the Laffer curve suggests this might not always be the case. When taxes are very high, people have less incentive to work and so economic output is restricted, lowering tax revenue. From this point, a reduction in the tax rate is outweighed by the increase in output that is stimulated, so increasing overall tax revenue. In practice, things aren't quite so simple and supply side policies often involve broader measures such as regulatory reform and privatization.

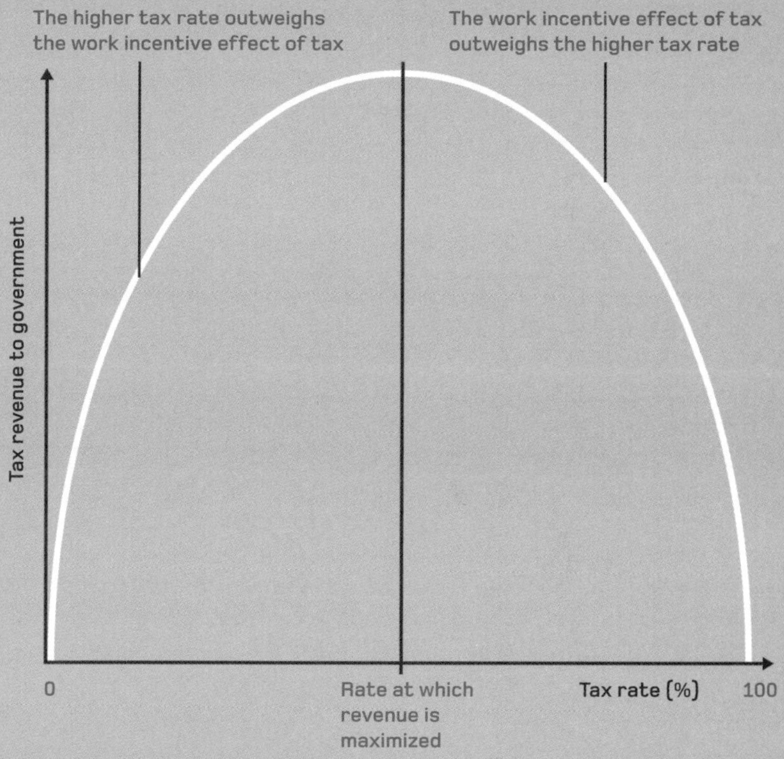
The higher tax rate outweighs the work incentive effect of tax
The work incentive effect of tax outweighs the higher tax rate
Tax revenue to government
0
Rate at which revenue is maximized
Tax rate (%)
100

Ricardian equivalence

A government can fund spending by borrowing or by raising taxes. Keynesians believe that governments can pull economies out of recessions by borrowing and then spending the proceeds. Purely tax-funded spending would not be effective because the spending boost would get offset by the tax hike. The theory of Ricardian equivalence, named after the 19th-century English economist David Ricardo (opposite), contradicts this reasoning: it says that the way a government finances its spending makes no difference. In particular, individuals will not respond to a boost in public spending funded by borrowing because they anticipate that the government will have to raise taxes later to repay its loans. Recent versions of the theory have shown that, for Ricardian equivalence to hold, people must be rational and make precise calculations about their future consumption and the likely impacts of government policies – conditions that are unlikely all to hold in practice. Nevertheless, the theory raises useful questions about the possible limits to government spending and borrowing.

Independent central banks and time inconsistency

In recent decades, many countries have elected to make their central banks independent. When central banks come under government control, monetary policies (interest rates and the money supply) are drawn up by politicians. Under independence these policies are set by a non-political committee of experts. The argument for independence comes from the insight that in achieving the aims of monetary policy, government is often its own worst enemy. Suppose that the government promises to keep inflation low. Such a promise is not credible because the government dislikes unemployment: it will end up boosting demand to reduce unemployment, and therefore pushing up inflation (see page 254). Individuals expect inflation to be higher, and anticipate that higher wages will be offset by higher prices, so the demand boost has no effect on unemployment: the outcome is just higher inflation. In this situation, the aim of low inflation is said to be 'time inconsistent'. Giving power to an independent committee that people believe to be committed to low inflation is one way of resolving the policy conflict.

Budget deficit and surplus

When a government spends more than it collects in taxes, it runs a budget deficit. When tax revenues exceed spending, it has a surplus. As an economy goes into recession, unemployment rises and welfare bills go up, while at the same time tax revenues fall as economic activity declines, so the budget tends to move into deficit. Conversely, during booms tax revenues are high and total welfare payments low, generating a surplus (see page 228).

The portion of the deficit caused by the economic cycle is the cyclical deficit. Over the cycle, such deficits should be offset by surpluses. The structural deficit, meanwhile, is the part of the deficit that goes beyond cyclical factors. It can arise if the government makes infrastructure investments that are not funded out of tax. Economists take different positions on the budget: some believe deficits are a useful way of fine-tuning the economy; others worry about the debt that builds up through continued deficits.

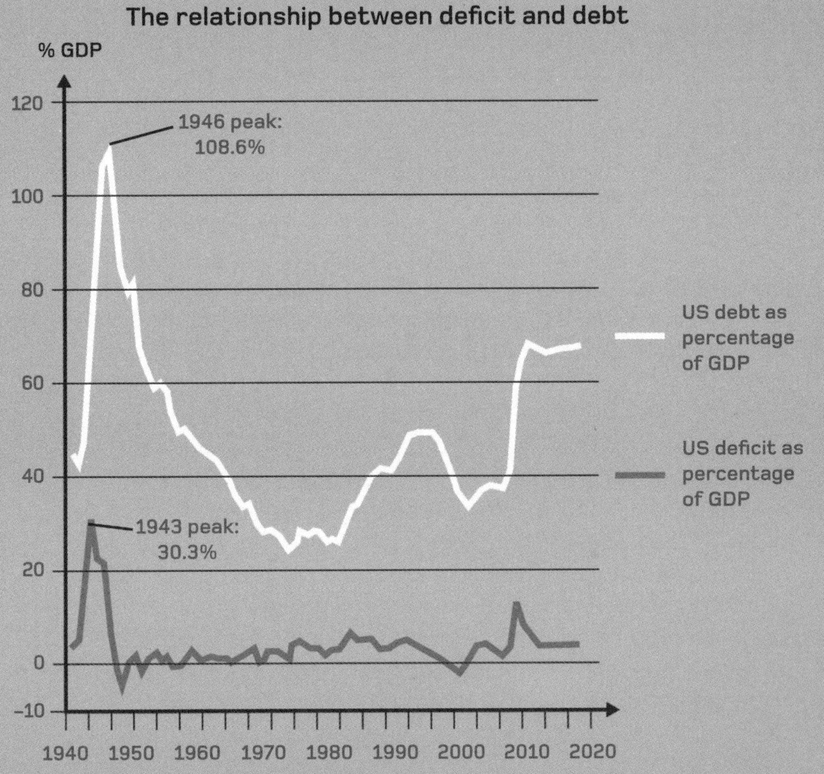
The relationship between deficit and debt
% GDP
120
100
80
60
40
20
0
–10
1946 peak:
108.6%
1943 peak:
30.3%
1940
1950
1960
1970
1980
1990
2000
2010
2020
US debt as
percentage
of GDP
US deficit as
percentage
of GDP

The balanced budget

Politicians often extol the virtues of 'balancing the budget', ensuring that government spending equals tax revenue so that there is no budget deficit or surplus. A strict version would have the budget balance in every year, but this is hard to achieve: the budget automatically goes into deficit during a downturn as the government has to spend more on unemployment benefits while collecting less in tax, reverting to surplus during periods of high growth.

Most economists would not advocate balancing the budget year by year. Some recommend balancing it 'over the cycle', meaning that apart from these cyclical effects the budget stays in balance. Deficits imply a build-up of debt that future generations have to repay. They mean that less resources are saved, leading to higher interest rates and lower investment. Other economists are much more sanguine about deficits, arguing that cuts to certain kinds of expenditure, such as health and education, might actually reduce growth.

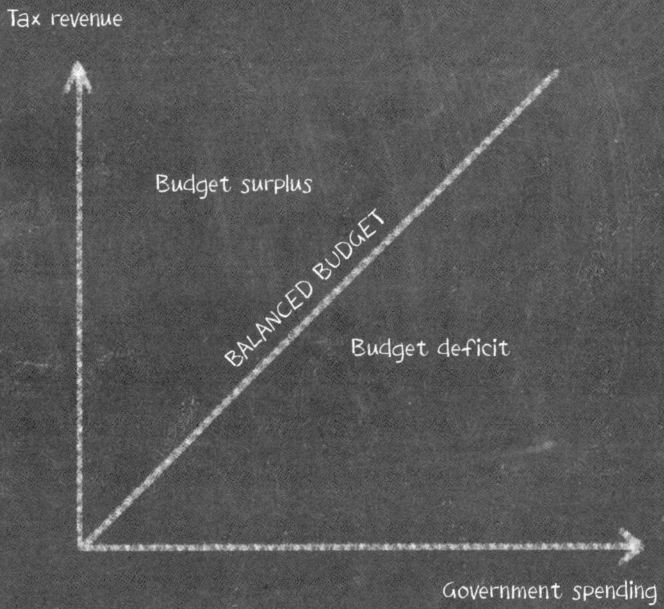
Tax revenue
Budget surplus
BALANCED BUDGET
Budget deficit
Government spending

Government debt

It is sometimes said that a country is like a person: it must live within its means and pay back its debts. One difference, though, is that an individual retires and dies, but a country produces indefinitely: this means that countries don't have to wipe clean their debts. A country's debt is sustainable when it can meet today's interest and other payment obligations, and it can do this if its debt stays at a reasonable proportion of GDP. As long as its economy expands over the long run, it can take on more debt.

Problems arise when the share of debt in GDP is so high that the government is unable to repay. Even before this, though, there are reasons to be concerned about the build-up of debt: it allows more consumption today, but less gets invested, hurting future generations. Some economists argue that debt doesn't even make individuals consume more today, because of their expectation of future tax rises. Too much debt may also stoke inflation, or damage a government's creditworthiness.

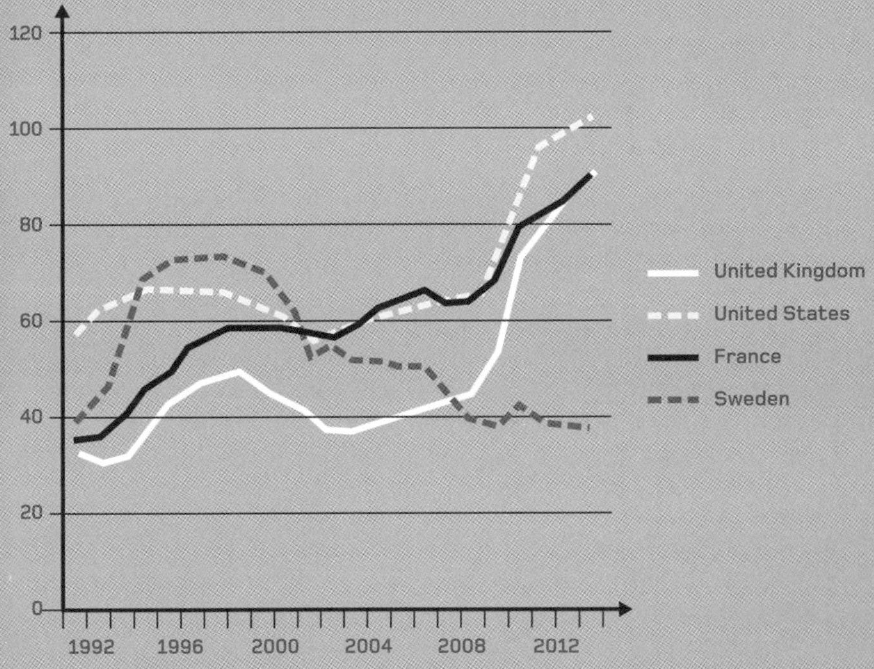

120
100
80
60
40
20
0
1992
1996
2000
2004
2008
2012
United Kingdom
United States
France
Sweden

Tax incidence

Tax incidence is the study of who ultimately bears the burden of a tax; this can be different from who formally pays the tax authorities. When people talk about companies passing on taxes to customers through higher prices, this is what they are referring to (see page 178). Suppose the government levies a tax on paint – the tax acts like a production cost, so it causes manufacturers to supply less paint. Lower supply in turn leads to a higher price, so both the buyer and the seller lose out: the seller doesn't sell as much and the buyers pay more. Suppose now that buyers are fairly insensitive to price changes, perhaps because there are few alternatives to using paint. If they are less sensitive to prices changes than the suppliers, they will be willing to bear more of the burden of the tax, so a larger share of the tax can be passed onto them without affecting demand too much. Conversely, if buyers are sensitive to price rises – perhaps they are willing to buy wallpaper instead of paint – then the seller will have to bear most of the tax impact.

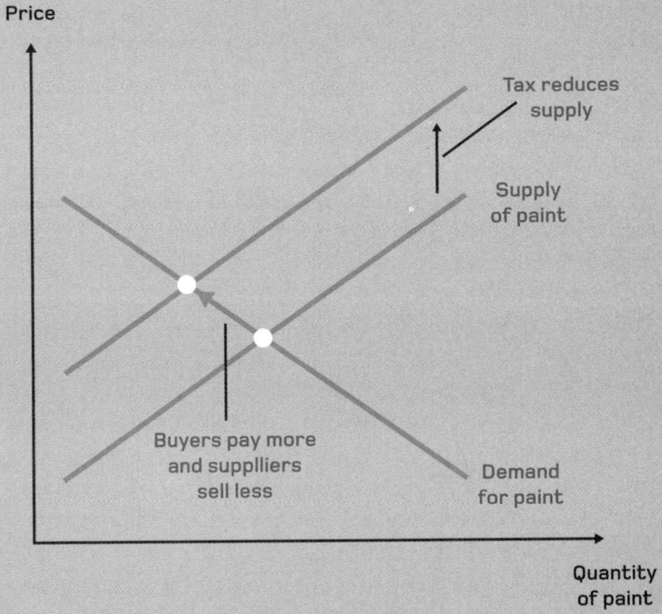
Price
Tax reduces
supply
Supply
of paint
Buyers pay more
and suppliers
sell less
Demand
for paint
Quantity
of paint

Direct and indirect taxation

A direct tax is imposed on particular individuals or companies who pay the tax authorities directly – you typically have no choice about whether to pay it. For example, workers pay income tax and companies pay taxes on their profits. Indirect taxes, meanwhile, aren't imposed on particular individuals. They are typically collected by intermediaries like a shop and then passed onto the government. The most common form of an indirect tax is a tax on transactions such as a sales tax, and by refraining from a purchase one wouldn't pay the tax.

It is sometimes argued that indirect taxes such as sales taxes are preferable to income taxes because taxes on labour discourage people from working. But even indirect taxes reduce real income by increasing prices, and taxes on some products rather than others distort the relative prices of goods, making markets work less efficiently. Indirect taxes are also criticized as 'regressive': lower income groups end up paying relatively more in tax as a share of their income.

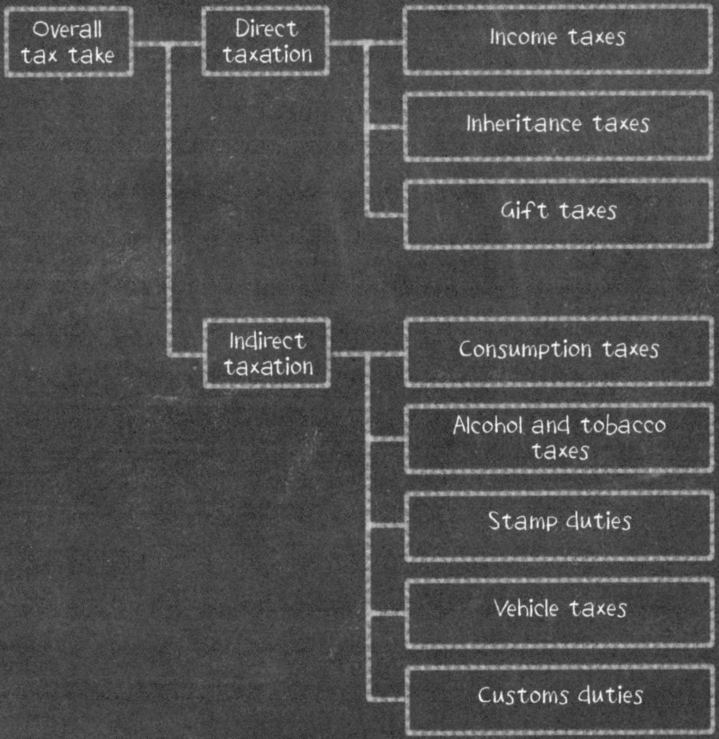
Overall tax take
Direct taxation
Income taxes
Inheritance taxes
Gift taxes
Indirect taxation
Consumption taxes
Alcohol and tobacco taxes
Stamp duties
Vehicle taxes
Customs duties

The deadweight loss of taxation

The benefits of taxation come with a cost, in terms of their interference with the market mechanism. Taxes on goods increase the prices of some goods relative to others, and income tax reduces workers' take-home wages, leading to so-called 'deadweight losses'.

Suppose that the government increases the income tax rate. This will reduce workers' disposable incomes, but increase the revenue for spending on public services. The higher rate makes some people work less, reducing their welfare, and the government doesn't gain any extra revenue to offset these lower hours. This is the deadweight loss to the economy. Incentive effects come from the marginal tax rate: this is the rate on an extra hour of work. When high, it may not be worth working more. Marginal rates tend to be lower at low income levels, so at high levels the average rate of tax – the share of total income that goes on tax – is often much less than the marginal rate.

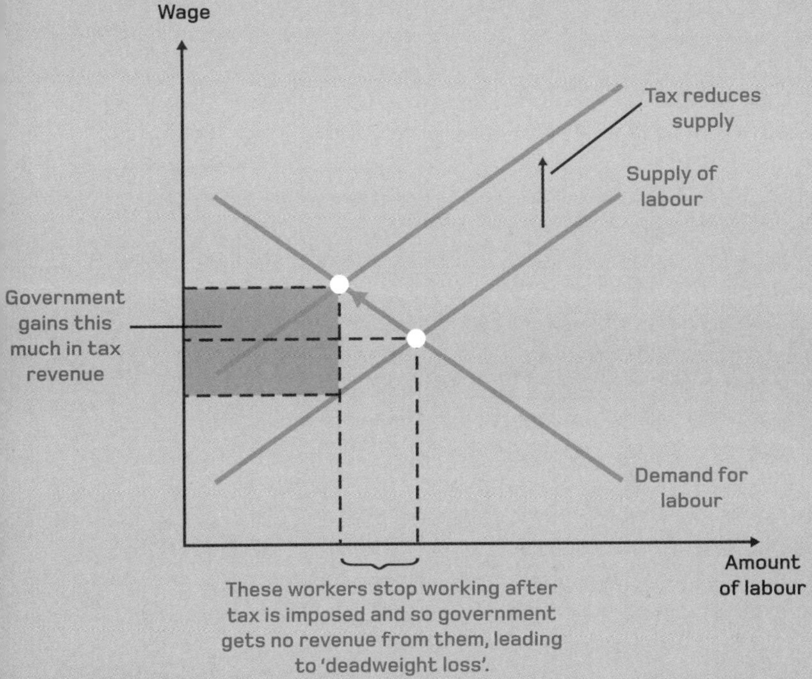
Wage
Tax reduces supply
Supply of labour
Government gains this much in tax revenue
Demand for labour
Amount of labour
These workers stop working after tax is imposed and so government gets no revenue from them, leading to 'deadweight loss'.

Lump-sum taxes

Economists view taxation as a necessary evil: people need governments, but taxes have incentive effects that hamper markets – income tax might make people work less, for example. Lump-sum taxes are fixed amounts to be paid by everyone regardless of income: they are an important kind of tax because they have no incentive effects. Because work decisions have no impact on my tax bill, I ignore the tax when deciding how much to work: the marginal tax – the rate of tax on extra work – for a lump-sum tax is zero.

In this sense, lump-sum taxes don't interfere with market incentives. However, the average rate – the share of total income paid in tax – for a lump-sum tax is higher at lower income levels, making them 'regressive' taxes. At an income of £10,000, a £1,000 lump-sum tax would imply an average rate of 10 per cent. At £1,000 income, the rate would be 100 per cent. The poor pay proportionately more, so although lump-sum taxes are efficient, many believe them to be unfair.

The UK government's introduction of a lump-sum tax in 1989–90 (dubbed the Poll Tax) sparked widespread protests at its perceived unfairness.

Redistributive taxation

In order to provide schools and hospitals, the government has to tax its population, but how should the burden of taxation be distributed? Economists often focus on the impact of taxation on economic efficiency: a fixed £500 tax on everyone is efficient because it doesn't influence how much people work, but such a tax might be considered unfair. Many argue that those with a greater ability to pay should contribute more.

All taxes redistribute income in some way, but redistributive taxation, as well as raising revenue also has a *goal* of making income distribution fairer. Progressive tax systems place a higher rate of tax on the rich, fulfilling the principle that those with greater ability to pay should contribute more, and also making distribution of income more equal. Under proportional systems, all taxpayers contribute the same fraction of income. Under regressive tax systems, even though the rich may pay more in absolute terms, they pay a lower fraction of their income than the poor.

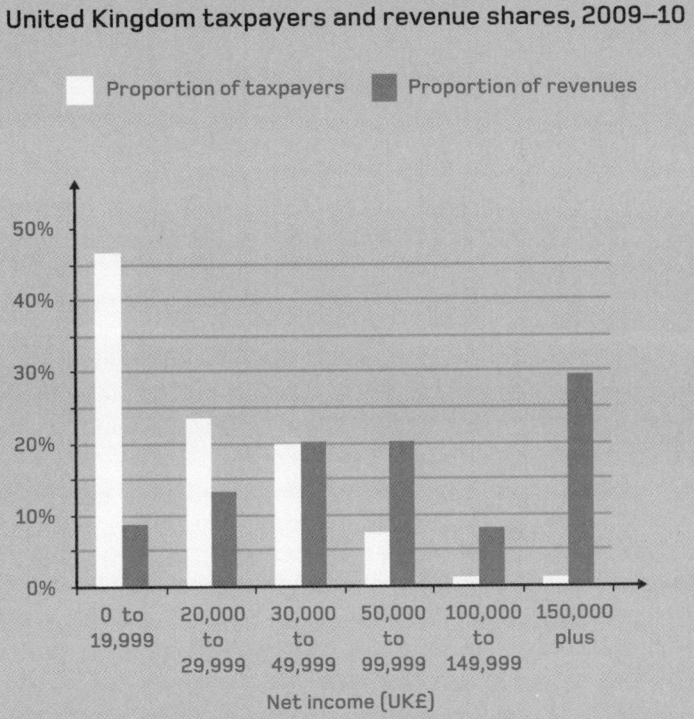
United Kingdom taxpayers and revenue shares, 2009–10
Proportion of taxpayers
Proportion of revenues
50%
40%
30%
20%
10%
0%
0 to 19,999
20,000 to 29,999
30,000 to 49,999
50,000 to 99,999
100,000 to 149,999
150,000 plus
Net income (UK£)

The welfare state

People inevitably lose jobs, get ill and become too old to work. To deal with these situations, governments fund health care and provide social security, paying a basic income to individuals who are unable to support themselves. Why can't private markets do the job by insuring people against ill health or unemployment? Economists now understand how imbalances of information between buyers and sellers mean that insurance markets often don't work very well. For example, because distinguishing between healthy and unhealthy people is difficult, insurers will take the very fact that a person asks for health insurance as an indication that he is unhealthy. This raises premiums and means that some people don't get insured. One rationale for social insurance or state provision of health care is to get around these market failures. The downside of such a 'welfare state' is that it may lead to adverse incentives. If health care is paid for, people might be less careful about their health, and the debate continues about the extent to which unemployment benefits encourage people to stay out of work.

FOODS SERV

Pensions

Economists think about an individual's earning, saving and consumption in terms of a life cycle: people earn and save when young, and use up their savings when old (see page 224). One way in which people save for their old age is through pensions. Governments provide a basic retirement income to the elderly – the state gets involved here in order to deal with problems inherent in the market provision of retirement incomes. On their own, individuals may find it difficult to plan income streams for decades ahead. It might be hard to get the necessary information and to know what to do with it.

Furthermore, private pension provision faces the problem that people may end up living for a long time, and individuals buying pensions are likely to be those who expect to live for a long time. Since this would cause a loss to the seller, private markets will tend to undersupply, suggesting another reason for state provision. Recently in the West, provision of pensions by employers, alongside the state, has become more common.

Price controls and subsidies

Governments sometimes restrict prices in key markets. Minimum wage laws place a floor on pay, while rent controls impose a ceiling on accommodation costs. Much of this is aimed at helping the poor, but by tinkering with demand- and supply-determined prices, controls have costs.

Suppose that a rent of £600 a month brings the supply of flats into line with demand: at £600 everyone demanding a flat can rent one. The government, however, then sets a rent ceiling of £500. Demand for flats rises and supply falls, so not everyone who wants a flat can get one. So flats have to be distributed by non-market means: perhaps those who are willing to wait the longest, or those with favourable personal connections obtain one. As time goes on, fewer new flats get built and the shortfall becomes even greater. The rent control helps those with flats, but shuts others out. Price floors have the opposite effect, leading to surpluses. Advocates of price controls argue that their social benefits outweigh these sorts of costs.

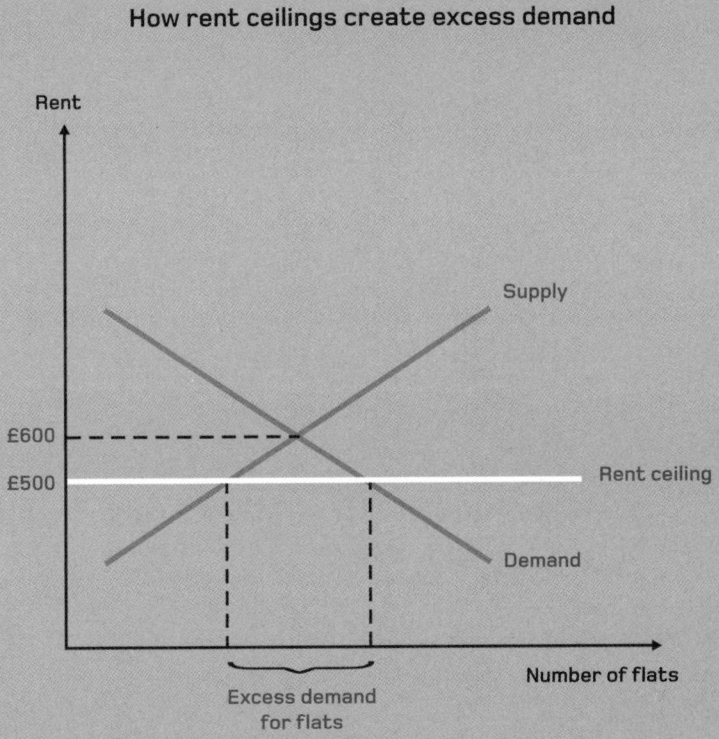
How rent ceilings create excess demand
Rent
Supply
£600
£500
Rent ceiling
Demand
Number of flats
Excess demand
for flats

Minimum wages

Since 1999 the United Kingdom has enforced a legal minimum wage. What are the arguments for and against such a measure? A minimum wage interferes with the normal functioning of the labour market, in which wages are determined by the supply and demand of labour. Legal minimum wages are usually a fraction of the average wage, so in most segments of the labour market they have no impact.

In low-wage sectors, however, the minimum wage bites. Where the imposition of a legal minimum does raise the wage, the supply of labour increases and the demand for it falls. Because more people are seeking work than offering it, unemployment results, and the wage is not allowed to adjust downwards to bring supply back into line with demand. For this reason, some economists criticize the use of minimum wages. Others argue that the the unemployment effect of the minimum wage is limited, and that any disadvantages from this are outweighed by the improved living standards of low-income workers.

Competition policy

Standard economics sees competition as leading to an efficient allocation of resources: when firms compete, they supply what consumers want at low prices. But often markets deviate from this ideal. The aim of competition (or anti-trust) policy is to *ensure* market competition. Suppose that Dairy Foods is contemplating a merger with Farmhouse Produce. Both are major suppliers of butter and if combined they would control 75 per cent of the butter market. The question for the competition authorities is whether this large market share would allow the merged firm to act like a monopoly and raise prices – if so, then it might forbid the merger. If there were products that consumers considered to be substitutes for butter – margarine perhaps – then the 75 per cent butter share would imply a lower degree of market power. Other anti-competitive practices that competition policy tries to counter include collusion between firms to fix prices in cartels (see page 168), and the predatory use of very low prices to drive competitors from the market (see page 172).

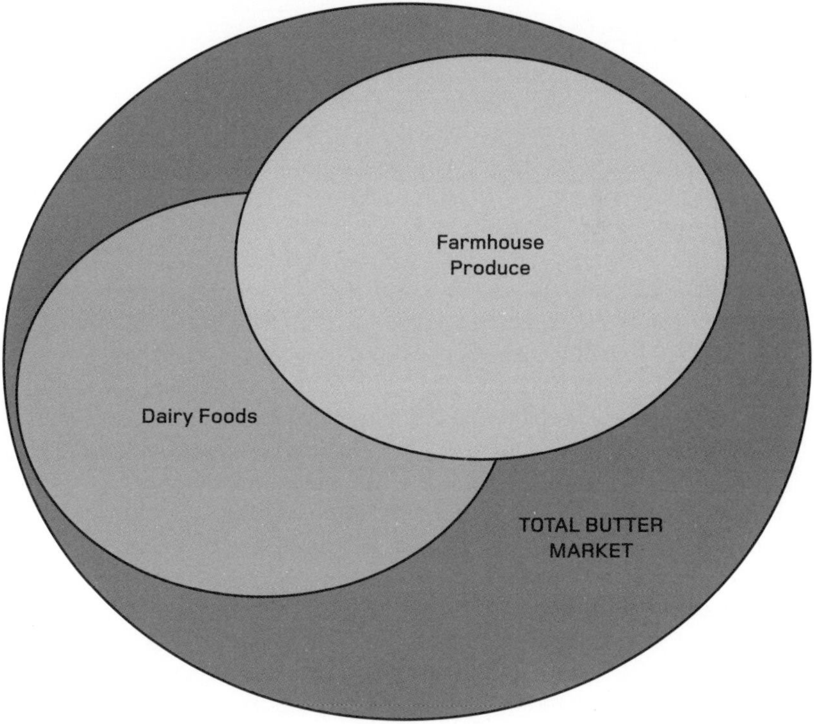
Farmhouse
Produce
Dairy Foods
TOTAL BUTTER
MARKET

Regulation

Even in market economies, governments regulate businesses where competition is absent. 'Natural monopolies', such as water suppliers, have average costs that decline as output rises because of large set-up investments. One large firm is cheaper than several firms operating different networks, but how do you stop the monopolist from charging high prices? The most efficient amount of water production is that for which the price – the value consumers place on the last unit of water – is equal to the cost of producing it (the marginal cost). To boost profits, monopolists produce less, charging more. The regulator could compel the water company to produce until price equals marginal cost. But at this high level of production, price becomes so low that the natural monopolist no longer covers average costs and makes a loss. One response to this problem is to subsidize the monopolist; an alternative is to set a price cap that allows the firm to remain viable. All of these solutions have drawbacks, so regulation is complex and often politically contentious.

Utilities such as the water supply are natural monopolies, and are therefore a good target for government regulation.

Taxing pollution

When the slurry by-product from a group of mines reduces the fertility of the surrounding soil so that adjacent nurseries produce less flowers, we have an 'externality' (see page 52). The slurry is a cost to society because it lowers flower production and the profit of the nurseries. However, the mines don't take this into account: they end up producing 'too much' coal and pollution. The government could compel the mines to produce less pollution. Alternatively, they could tax pollution, charging the mines for every tonne of slurry produced.

Such a pollution tax is set at a level that takes into account all the costs and benefits to society. It makes the mines face the social cost of their activities where market prices didn't, in a sense 'internalizing' the externality. Taxes allow the polluters to respond in various ways: some may find it easy to pollute less, but for others this could prove very costly, so they reduce it less and pay more tax. Overall, this can lead to an efficient distribution of pollution-reduction efforts among the mines.

Valuing human life

Should a council hire an extra lifeguard for its swimming pool? To decide, the council has to compare the salary costs with the benefits in terms of lives saved. But how can one express the value of a life in money – surely life is priceless? Because resources are scarce, putting an infinite value on life leads to an absurdity: it might require the council to spend unlimited amounts on safety, to hire hundreds of lifeguards, install advanced CCTV cameras and build a poolside medical centre. Eventually resources would be taken away from schools, hospitals and rubbish collection. In reality, pools are staffed only to reduce risks to a reasonable level.

Economists argue that there must be an implicit value placed on lives to determine how much safety is worthwhile. They compute life values by seeing how much people are willing to pay to eliminate risks. One way is to look at the difference in wages between risky and less risky jobs. Some studies have estimated the value of life in the US at around US$7 million.

Comparative advantage

Suppose that France is better at making cheese, England at beer. If France specializes in cheese and England in beer and the two countries trade, then both gain: the French get cheaper beer, the English cheaper cheese. The theory of comparative advantage shows that even if England was worse at both goods, there are still gains from specialization and trade. Suppose that to make an extra keg of beer, England has to give up two wheels of cheese output, while France would have to give up three wheels of cheese to make an extra keg. England has a comparative advantage in beer production because the 'cost' of extra beer in terms of cheese is less than for France. This can be the case even if in absolute terms France is better at making both goods. Both countries can still gain if England specializes in beer and France in cheese. What determines countries' comparative advantage? The availability of capital and labour in a country is one factor, although how countries build up comparative advantage in the longer term is a more complex story.

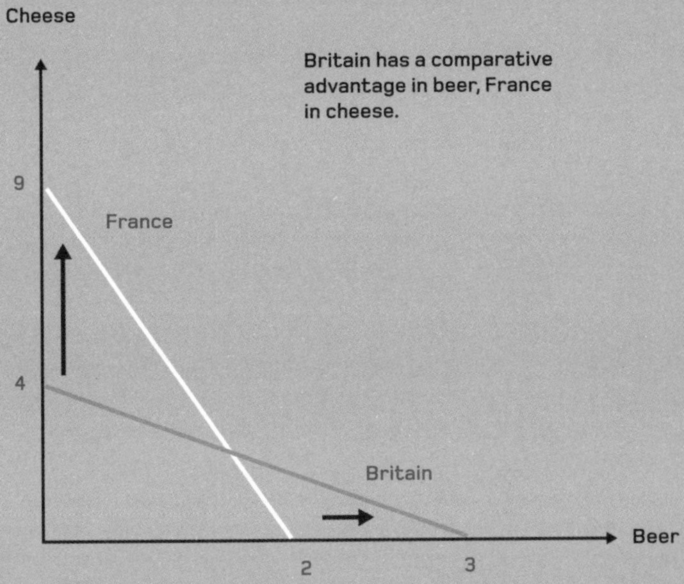
Cheese
Britain has a comparative advantage in beer, France in cheese.
9
France
4
Britain
Beer
2
3

The balance of payments

A country's balance of payments is a record of payments and receipts between its firms and individuals and those of other countries. The balance of payments always balances: *total* payments equal *total* receipts, and only components of the overall balance of payments can be in deficit or surplus. For example, if the US exports £10 million worth of mobile phones to Britain and Britain sells nothing to the US, then Britain has a 'trade deficit' of £10 million, but US businesses now hold an extra £10 million of British assets, representing a surplus on the 'capital account' – the segment of the balance of payments that records capital flows between countries.

People often worry about trade deficits: they can arise if domestic goods are not internationally competitive due to the low productivity of domestic firms. However, there are many reasons for trade deficits, and not all of them are bad: for instance, a country might be growing fast, building lots of roads and so importing large volumes of tarmac and steel.

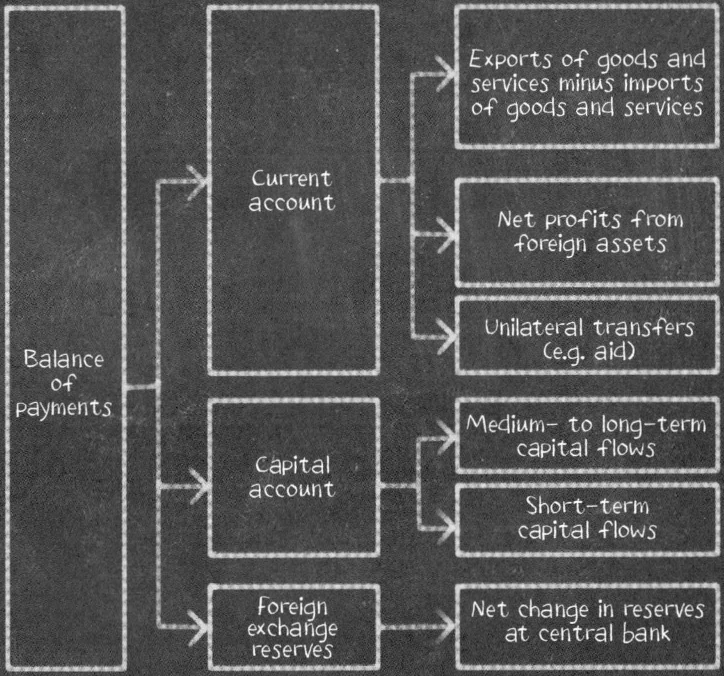
Balance of payments
Current account
Exports of goods and services minus imports of goods and services
Net profits from foreign assets
Unilateral transfers (e.g. aid)
Capital account
Medium- to long-term capital flows
Short-term capital flows
Foreign exchange reserves
Net change in reserves at central bank

Free trade

Free trade happens when countries open up their markets to foreign goods through the removal of tariffs and quotas on imports or the repeal of laws and regulations that hinder trade. Most economists welcome free trade, since it brings the expansion of markets and competition.

An early step towards free trade was taken by Britain in 1846 when it abolished the 'Corn Laws' protecting British farmers from foreign competition. Since then, free trade has waxed and waned, retreating between the wars, advancing again in the latter part of the 20th century. Sometimes free trade is served through bilateral agreements between countries, sometimes through multilateral treaties such as those of the World Trade Organization. Some economists question the consensus that free trade is always a good thing, pointing out that it can hurt some groups of workers, and that countries at early stages of development might need some protection from foreign competition to expand their industries.

While the Corn Laws protected British famers from foreign competition, they also limited supply and kept prices high, forcing working people to spend a substantial amount of their income on staples. Huge rallies were held as part of the campaign for abolition.

Protectionism and trade wars

Economic theory says that there are great gains to be had from trade. When two countries specialize in particular goods and engage in trade, both are better off. Protectionism is a policy under which countries close themselves off from international trade, often by putting tariffs (taxes) or quotas on foreign imports. Because these policies unravel the gains from trade, most economists argue that they are economically damaging. Often there are calls for protectionism during times of economic crisis: the hope is that growth and employment can be maintained by insulating the domestic economy from foreign competition. The problem is that trading partners may try similar policies themselves, sparking a trade war and eventually leading to lower trade and income in both countries, as happened during the Great Depression of the 1930s. Some economists argue that temporary, targeted protection can be useful to help countries develop 'infant industries' that need to be cushioned from foreign competition until they are efficient enough to compete internationally.

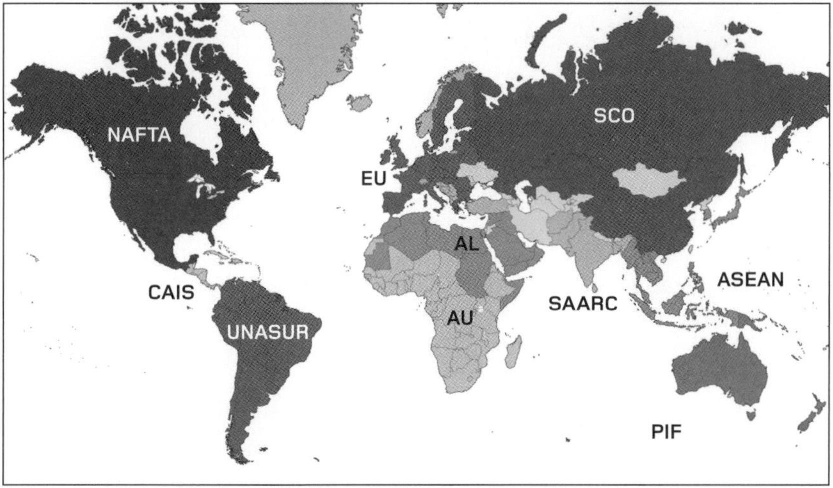

Major global trading blocs

AL: Arab League
ASEAN: Association of Southeast Asian Nations
AU: African Union
CAIS: Central American Integration System
EU: European Union
NAFTA: North American Free Trade Agreement
PIF: Pacific Islands Forum
SAARC: South Asian Association for Regional Cooperation
SCO: Shanghai Cooperation Organization
UNASUR: Union of South American Nations

Globalization and market integration

Globalization can be a confusing, woolly term. From an economist's point of view, it is about the integration of markets that were previously separated by geography. Globalization is enhanced when English potatoes and French potatoes compete for the same consumers in England and France, where before they were only bought and sold in their countries of origin. An indication of economic globalization, then, is the equalization of prices of goods in different places – potatoes in London and in Paris.

Globalization occurs when transport costs become low enough to make it profitable to trade. The development of shipping and railways in the 19th century was a major spur. Governments can assist the process by cutting tariffs, or hinder it by raising them. Since the Second World War, globalization of markets for goods and services has proceeded apace. Financial globalization has also progressed. Labour migration is another, politically charged component of globalization.

Trade and geography

Economists have recently started to think of industrial specialization and patterns of international trade as arising more or less by accident. The classical theory of trade says that one country becomes the leading exporter of cloth because it is abundant in sheep, another of wine because it has the right weather. In fact, a lot of trade goes on between industrialized economies with essentially similar natural resources and populations.

However, an industry like steel production is much more efficient at a large scale, because of the big investments in plant and machinery that initially have to be made. So once one country starts producing steel it builds up a cost advantage. This makes it hard for other countries to catch up, so the country comes to dominate steel exports. Some other country might just as well have been the first to set up a steel plant, in which case it would have become the leading producer.

ACME
MOTORS
WORLD OF
STEEL

Fair trade

The aim of fair trade organizations is to funnel more of the gains from international trade to producers in developing countries. Consider a jar of coffee in the supermarket: fair trade advocates point out that the revenues of the Ethiopian coffee farmer from the sale of the beans that went into the jar form only a fraction of the supermarket price – the rest consists of the costs and profit margins of intermediaries.

When the farmer joins a fair trade scheme, he is guaranteed a minimum price, in return for which he has to adhere to labour and environmental standards. His coffee is sold under a fair trade certification. Western consumers who value fair trade aims are willing to pay a bit more for the coffee. The hope is that such measures smooth the fluctuations in income faced by small farmers in poor countries as the market prices of crops move up and down. However, the fair trade movement can be criticized: some argue that it does not help the poorest, who are predominantly casual labourers rather than farmers.

The Bretton Woods system

During the Great Depression of the 1930s, many countries shut out foreign imports to protect domestic markets, leading to a disintegration of the international economy. A 1944 conference at Bretton Woods, New Hampshire, laid the foundations for rebuilding global cooperation. Countries' exchange rates were tied to the US dollar. The International Monetary Fund and World Bank were set up to help governments with financing and economic development. Another aim was to reverse protectionism. The General Agreement on Tariffs and Trade (GATT), later to become the World Trade Organization, oversaw rounds of international trade negotiations that continue to the present.

The system presided over several decades of stable growth, but ended in the early 1970s, after which the world saw increased economic instability. In the wake of the recent financial crisis, some commentators, evoking Bretton Woods, have argued for a another remodelling of the international finanscial system.

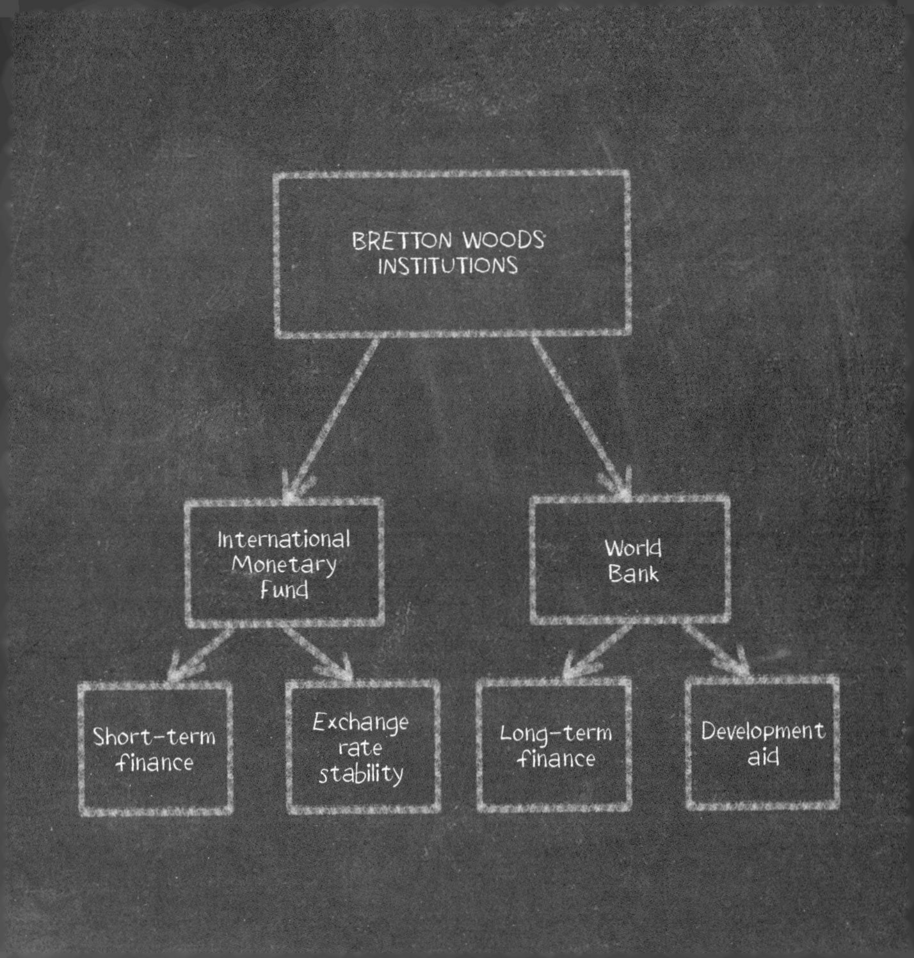
BRETTON WOODS INSTITUTIONS
International Monetary Fund
World Bank
Short-term finance
Exchange rate stability
Long-term finance
Development aid

The US trade deficit and global imbalances

As the largest economy in the world, the United States has run a 'trade deficit' for many years, importing more than it exports. Such deficits have to be funded by capital flows from abroad. The large US deficit, and corresponding inflow of foreign money, are global imbalances in the international trading system. Such imbalances are a fact of economic life and don't necessarily pose problems, but the size and persistence of today's imbalances worry commentators, some of whom argue that they fed into the recent financial crisis. The US trade deficit has been mirrored by Chinese surpluses that generated a flow of capital to the rest of the world and contributed to a global 'savings glut'. These savings flooded Western financial markets, leading to a boom in lending, some of which went into the overly liberal mortgage lending (see page 128) that went on to undermine financial markets. The size of the US trade deficit remains controversial – some are concerned that if capital flows decline, it will become unsustainable and the economy will suffer a major shock.

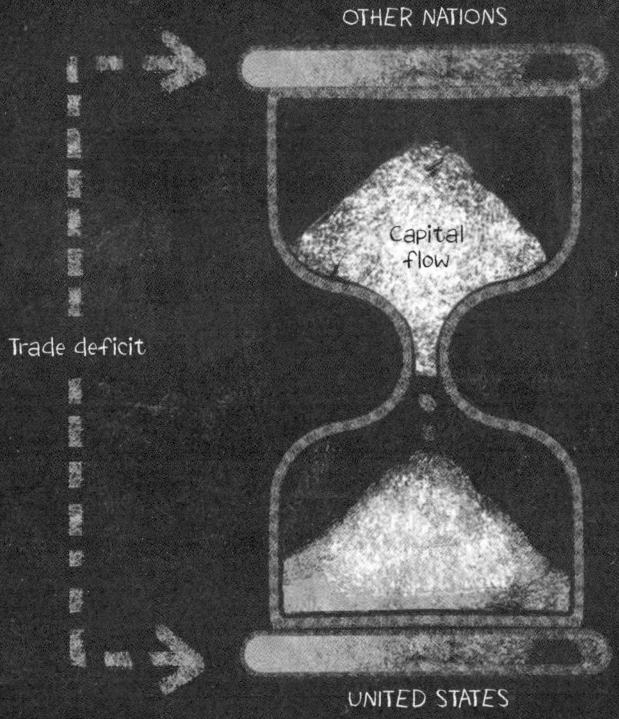
OTHER NATIONS
Capital flow
Trade deficit
UNITED STATES

International capital flows

In the last few decades, the flow of capital between countries has grown much faster than world economic output. Capital moves to a country when someone buys its shares or bonds or makes direct investments in its firms. Most capital moves between advanced industrial nations, but a few developing nations attract some of it. Without foreign capital, a country can only invest the money that its citizens save: capital inflows relieve this constraint, enhancing growth potential.

Measures by a country to open its economy to foreign investment are known as capital liberalization. For developing nations especially, the benefits of such policies have been patchier than economic models might suggest, and some even blame it for the increased prevalence of financial crises in the developing world. It could be that different kinds of capital flows have different impacts: for example, some studies suggest that direct investment in a country's businesses has more of an effect on growth than loans.

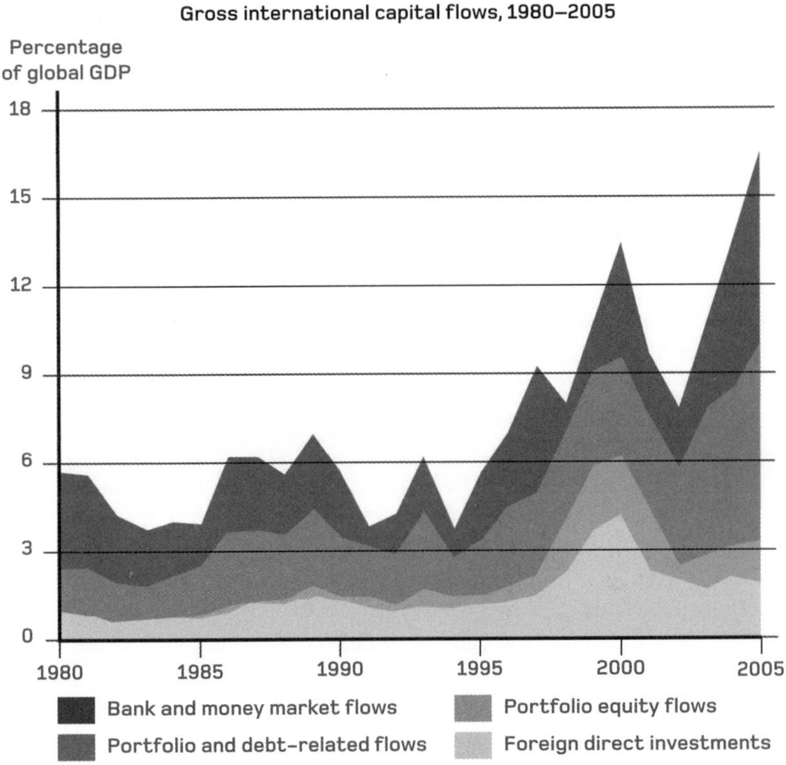
Gross international capital flows, 1980–2005
Percentage of global GDP
18
15
12
9
6
3
0
1980
1985
1990
1995
2000
2005
Bank and money market flows
Portfolio equity flows
Portfolio and debt-related flows
Foreign direct investments

Multinational firms

Multinational firms are those which operate factories and offices in different countries. Their rise has been an important part of the globalization of markets (see page 310). Why do firms need to run their own operations in countries where they wish to sell? Suppose that British Pills Incorporated wants to launch a new drug in India: it could simply produce the drug in the UK and export it. There might, however, be advantages to producing in India, such as the availability of cheaper raw materials and labour. Even so, why not license an Indian firm to produce the drug? One reason is that British Pills might have a 'firm specific asset', perhaps a special production method or drug formula. The asset's value would decline if it gave access to another firm – it might soon be used to make a competing product. A better option would be for British Pills to set up its own operations in India. Multinationals' decisions about where to locate overseas facilities are influenced by factors including market size, local production costs, tax levels and the legal environment.

Labour migration

Labour migration is an important facet of the development of markets. When countries industrialize, workers move from rural to urban areas, attracted by the higher wages offered by industrial enterprises. A similar phenomenon happens internationally: huge numbers of migrants flowed to the New World during the 19th century and international migration has remained important ever since. As with internal migration, economists stress the role of wage gaps between different countries in generating international migration: migrants flow from low-wage to high-wage countries. Eventually one might see a levelling off, if wages begin to equalize across countries. In practice, migration is a far more complex phenomenon than simple economic models suggest. All sorts of cultural and social factors are involved, and the issue has become highly politicized. Nevertheless, even basic economics can be useful here, if only to remind us that labour migration is as much a part of the logic of globalization as the expansion of international markets for goods and finance.

Real and nominal exchange rates

Exchange rates – the cost of converting pounds into US dollars, for example – are determined by the demand and supply of different currencies. They mediate any interaction between buyers and sellers of goods and services in different countries. The nominal exchange rate is that displayed on a bank's list of rates – US$1 equaling UK£0.65, for example.

However, this nominal exchange rate doesn't tell you what you could actually buy in a foreign country with your own money. By taking account of countries' price levels, the real exchange rate measures this. It might tell you how much British apples cost in terms of American apples. Britain's real exchange rate goes up when its nominal rate rises, but also if its goods get more expensive, or American goods get cheaper. A fall in Britain's real exchange rate means that its goods have become cheaper compared to other countries. This encourages consumers at home and abroad to buy more British goods.

GBP/CHF

Fixed and floating exchange rate systems

Systems of exchange rates lie on a spectrum between fixed and floating. In a pure floating exchange rate system, the price of one currency in terms of another arises out of market supply and demand for the currency – the price of the currency tends to rise when demand for it goes up or supply falls.

In contrast, an exchange rate is fixed when a set rate is maintained: for example, the Argentinian government might fix its exchange rate at two pesos to the US dollar. There are also intermediate arrangements, such as the establishment of exchange-rate bands within which a currency is allowed to fluctuate. A fixed exchange rate binds a country's monetary policy – its control over money supply and interest rates – because this has to be consistent with the specified rate. Compared to a floating exchange rate, there is less freedom to alter monetary policy in response to domestic economic conditions. Some, however, argue that fixed exchange rates can enhance economic stability.

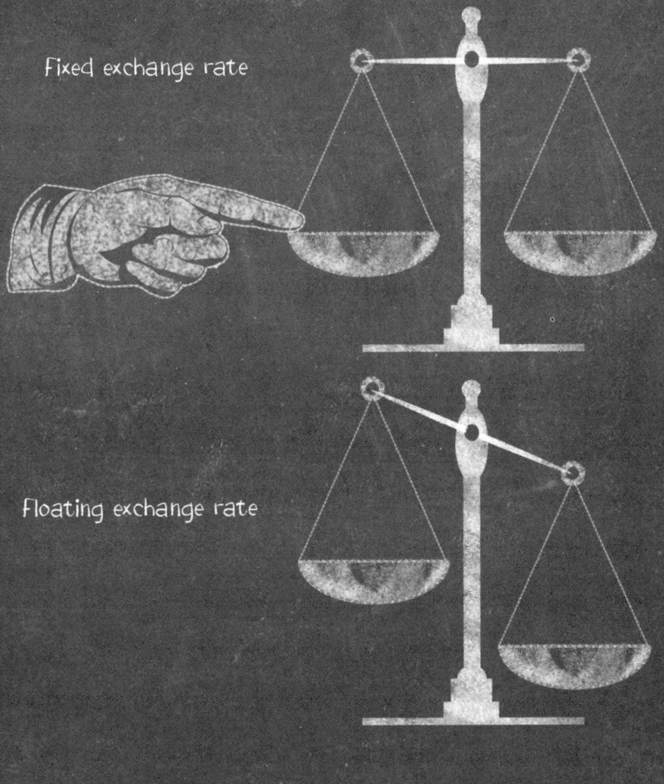
Fixed exchange rate
Floating exchange rate

The gold standard

Under the gold standard, gold is used as currency – or more commonly, paper currency can be converted into gold. The gold standard was in use in the early part of the 20th century and some look back on it with nostalgia, believing it to have enhanced the stability of the international monetary system. Under the gold standard, currencies are given a set value in terms of gold. This means that their values in terms of other currencies – their exchange rates – are also fixed. When this works well, it can reduce trading uncertainties. It can also hold governments to the maintenance of price stability because the authorities cannot easily expand a money supply that has to be backed by the gold to honour it. However, at other times this can act as a straitjacket on economies: during the Great Depression it limited the ability of governments to stimulate their economies through expansion of the money supply, prolonging the downturn. While many economists value price discipline and stable currencies, few would now advocate a return to a traditional gold standard.

250g
Fine Gold
999.9

Currency crises

Since the 1970s, currency crises have become increasingly common. Crises occur when a currency starts to get sold in large amounts, depressing its value. If the currency is 'fixed' (maintained at a particular rate), then that rate has to be abandoned in what is known as a devaluation. One type of crisis happens when there is a conflict between the exchange rate and other areas of economic policy. Suppose a government is spending more than it collects in taxes: if it finances the difference by increasing the money supply, this lowers the value of its currency. To maintain the exchange rate, the government must then use foreign exchange reserves to buy its own currency. Eventually, though, the government runs out of reserves and the currency has to be devalued. Other theories of currency crisis suggest that they may be self-fulfilling: many people worrying about the strength of the currency can be enough to trigger sell-offs and a crisis. Currency crises in developing countries over recent decades, meanwhile, were precipitated by a sudden drying-up of foreign capital inflows.

Single currencies

A single world currency would surely be too tight a constraint on so many diverse economies, while separate currencies for every town would hopelessly complicate economic life. For historical reasons, most currencies have evolved within borders, but many European countries have recently opted for a single, shared currency – the euro. If currencies don't have to coincide with national borders, then what is the optimal coverage of a currency? When trading partners share a single currency, they reduce currency conversion costs and boost trade. However, a country with its own currency sets its own monetary policy (the level of money supply and interest rates) – power that it gives up under a single currency. In the case of the euro, monetary policy is decided by the European Central Bank. This works well when the economic cycles of member states are synchronized, but problems arise if countries need different monetary policies, as happened in the wake of the economic crisis that began in 2008. Questions are now being asked about whether Europe really is an optimal currency area.

1
EURO

Exchange rate depreciation

If the pound was worth $2.50 last week, but $2.30 today, its value has fallen: the pound has depreciated, the dollar appreciated. When the exchange rate can move freely, what determines its level? In simple terms, the price of a currency is like that for pens: it is determined by supply and demand. A country with high inflation will tend to see a depreciating exchange rate, because the currency's purchasing power falls. Higher interest rates will tend to draw in foreign capital and cause the exchange rate to rise. The exchange rate is also influenced by the level of imports and exports: the trade deficit that occurs when a country's imports exceed exports causes depreciation of its currency. This can be helpful, however, because it makes domestic goods more internationally competitive and helps to boost exports. In modern globalized capital markets, investors' perceptions about the riskiness of putting money into countries have their own impacts on the exchange rate: political instability can deter investors and lead to declines in currencies' values.

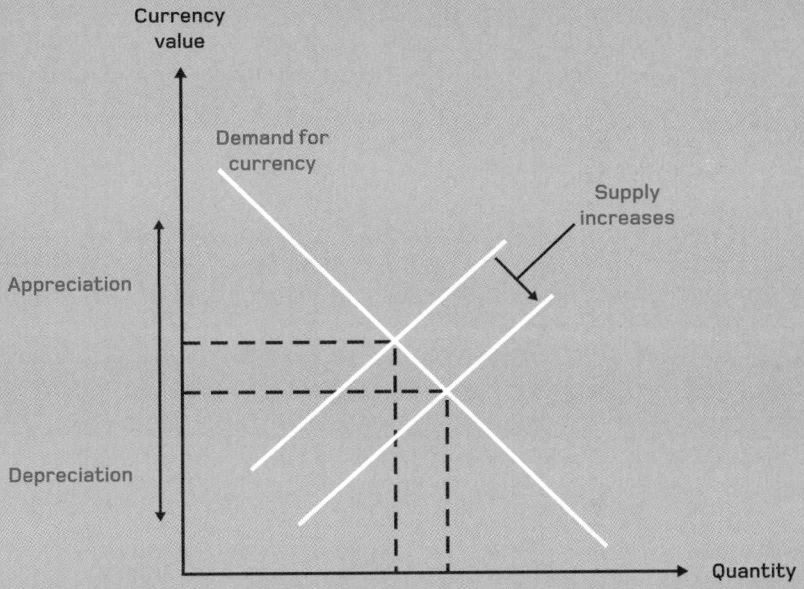

For a given level of demand, an increase in the supply of currency will lead to a depreciation in the market value

Economics and ethics

The founders of economics – figures such as Adam Smith and John Stuart Mill (opposite) – were philosophers: their work fused ethical enquiry with economic analysis. Since their time, however, economics and moral philosophy have become much less connected. Modern economics, with its mathematical models and sophisticated statistics, is often viewed as an objective, scientific discipline dealing with hard-nosed realities. In contrast, ethics is seen as subjective, not amenable to scientific analysis and existing in a wholly separate realm. Perhaps the central question of economics, however, is how to allocate scarce resources among individuals with conflicting desires. The question of whether to build more hospitals, universities or shopping centres has a strong ethical dimension, and many thinkers have continued to be interested in the interaction between economics and ethics. Recent studies of individual economic behaviour have found that it is driven as much by moral beliefs such as principles of fairness as it is by economic calculation.

Religion and the economy

Economists have become increasingly interested in the way that social norms and beliefs – including religion – influence countries' economic fortunes. Religious organizations can be viewed as a kind of 'social capital' (see page 366) – networks and relationships between individuals that may be economically beneficial. On the other hand, religious restrictions, such as those on the participation of women in the labour market, can hinder market expansion. German sociologist and economist Max Weber was one of the first to look at the implications of religious belief for economic performance. He famously argued that Protestantism propelled economic development in Europe by making hard work virtuous. Thrift and profit-making became an article of faith, so Weber argued, and encouraged the rise of capitalism. More recently, economists have tried to explain the rise of certain Asian countries through 'Asian-values' or Confucianism. At a theoretical level, many of these ideas remain speculative, and empirically disentangling the impacts of religion in different societies is fraught with difficulty.

Economics and culture

Which comes first, economics or culture? If you sell your old stereo to a friend, you might offer him a knock-down price because there is an expectation that friends do each other favours. You probably also exchange gifts with friends. Such behaviours affect the allocation of economic resources, but seem to be culturally driven. Economists view individuals as rational profit maximizers – but if so, why don't they try to get the best 'price' out of their friends and waste less money on presents? Austrian economist and anthropologist Karl Polanyi argued that economic organization is determined by a society's culture and social norms rather than by economic rationality, particularly in traditional societies. Even in modern economies, culture influences economic life. A conventional economist might argue that beneath the apparently culturally driven behaviour lies hard-nosed economic calculation: I help you only so that you help me, and what really matters is still profit and return. Polanyi, on the other hand, argued that customs are entirely distinct from the pursuit of profit.

If people are economically rational, why do they give presents?

Institutions and property rights

The buying and selling of goods requires property rights, and if people don't have confidence that such rights will be respected, economic activity is likely to be hampered. Analysis of the fundamental prerequisites for economic life, including these rights, is essential to understanding the creation of wealth. Property rights are what economists call an institution – a 'rule of the game' that governs the economic activities of individuals, firms and governments. These rules can be formal laws and regulations or informal social norms and customs.

Institutional economists have tended to stress the importance of property rights as essential to creating incentives to trade, to invest and to innovate. Political instability and rapacious governments damage property rights. At the same time, the rise of the state has gone with the growth of markets. So identifying the mix of institutions that brings prosperity is a difficult and as yet uncompleted task, and what helps in one country or era may be a hindrance in others.

Marxist economics

For Karl Marx, capitalism was a dynamic and innovative economic system, an advance on the earlier feudal economy. However, he argued it contained flaws that would eventually lead to its collapse. Under capitalism, capital owners hire workers, and Marx said that the value of a good resides in the labour used to make it. For capitalists to earn profit, they must extract a surplus above this value – hence workers get exploited through low wages and the threat of unemployment. Profits are also driven by technology and the division of labour: under capitalism the worker no longer produces a rug in his cottage, but spends his days loading spools onto factory looms. This is 'alienated labour': capitalist work saps people's creativity and undermines human connection. Marx predicted that conflict between workers and capitalists would eventually lead to the overthrow of capitalism and establishment of communism. Despite the collapse of the communist states, elements of Marx's thinking and his linking of the economic, social and political spheres remain influential to this day.

The labour theory of value

Until the 19th century, it was believed that the value of goods came from the labour used to make them: a chair that took 50 hours of labour was worth ten times as much as a stool that took five. Even the value of goods made in factories could be traced to labour. A factory-made chair is produced by machines operated by people. The machines are made by other labourers, and the iron used to make the machines is produced by still others. The labour theory of value became closely associated with Karl Marx – he asked how profits were possible if the value of goods came from labour. Marx argued that capitalists were able to exploit the workers and squeeze a surplus out of them (see page 346).

From the 19th century, economists moved on from the labour theory of value. It was seen that a dress that took ten hours to make was not necessarily worth five times more than a diamond that took two hours to cut. Value was determined by people's desires, and in the market by supply and demand.

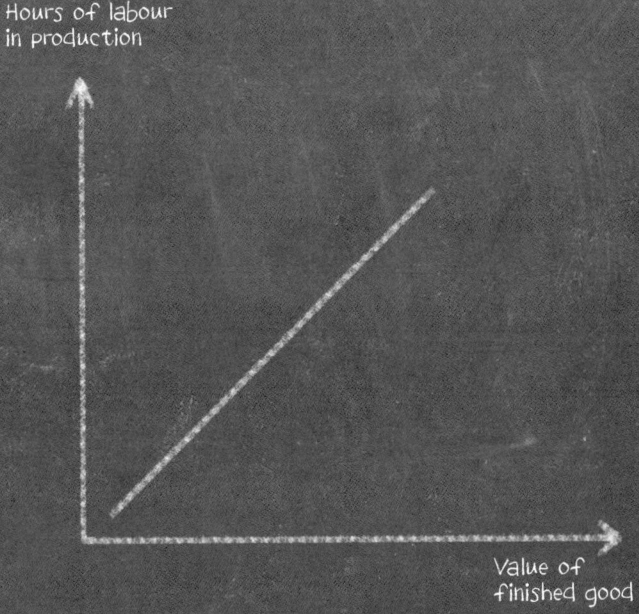
Hours of labour
in production
Value of
finished good

Central planning

With the advent of communism, economic thinkers began comparing the workings of socialist and market-based systems. A long-standing tenet of economics was that market prices lead to an efficient allocation of resources: if lots of people want bicycles, the price of bicycles will rise, encouraging more production. In socialist systems, central planners decide what should be produced. Some argued that they, too, would be able to bring about an efficient allocation of goods, essentially replicating what markets do while reducing their inequities. The Austrian economist, Ludwig von Mises denied this possibility – only through interplay of supply and demand in markets could prices emerge reflecting society's true valuation of different goods. The sheer complexity of economies with thousands of different goods and services would be too much for any central planner, he argued, and the result would be large inefficiencies and errors in matching what people wanted with what was produced. This was certainly one of the problems that the communist states eventually ran into.

ПАРТИЯ

The social market

When Tony Blair came to power in Britain in 1997, there was much talk of a 'Third Way', a middle ground between left- and right-wing approaches to economic management. In fact, the attempt to create a synthesis of left and right goes back to the immediate postwar period, when economists proposed the model known as the social market economy.

Subsequently established in many European countries, the social market combined private enterprise with government provision of goods and services such as health and schooling. The state also created 'safety nets' – unemployment benefits, pensions and other payments aimed at mitigating the social impact of markets. Many governments had tax policies that redistributed wealth from the rich to the poor. The idea was to harness the productive, dynamic aspects of capitalism, while tempering them with socialist principles of equality and fairness. Today, most European economies combine markets with state intervention.

Trade unions

The textbook model of a labour market involves millions of workers making their own contracts with millions of employers. However, with the rise of industrial capitalism, the employers often become large corporations. An important function of trade unions is to increase workers' bargaining power against these powerful employers. By negotiating collectively, and agreeing not to compete with each other, workers can achieve better pay. Employers may even prefer to deal with unions, as it simplifies setting wages and conditions. The role of unions is more complex than this, however, as they mediate other interactions between workers and employers.

Unions have come in for criticism from some economists, who argue that while they ensure higher wages for union members, they shut out non-unionized workers and create unemployment. In recent decades, many governments attempted to reduce the power of unions, believing them to be an impediment to the modernization of economies.

BLIC AND COMMERCIAL
SERVICES UNION
ORTH WEST
REGION
EQUALITY
pcs
UNITY
SOLIDARITY
RKERS OF THE
Yorkshire Branch
pcs
pcs
Ministry of Defence
...invest in housing and transport
pcs
Defending Jobs and Services
...don't cut jobs or public services
don't
enew
rident
UNISON

Shortages and rationing

In properly functioning markets, supply equals demand. There are no shortages: anyone willing to pay the market price can obtain the good. In contrast, Hungarian economist Janos Kornai showed why shortages arise in centralized economies.

In standard markets, firms are subject to 'hard budget constraints' – they must earn enough revenue to cover costs. This ensures they produce as efficiently as possible, making as much as they can with the smallest inputs. Kornai argued that in centrally planned economies, firms face 'soft budget constraints': if they make losses, they get bailed out by the state. As a result, they don't have an incentive to economize on inputs or produce in quantity. As they eat up inputs without increasing production, shortages emerge, until eventually consumers are forced to queue for goods. Even in capitalist economies, not all budget constraints are hard: some firms considered 'too big to fail' are still bailed out by the taxpayer, as some banks were in the wake of the 2007–8 financial crisis.

Economic liberalism

Two of the dominant economic thinkers of the 20th century were Friedrich Hayek (opposite) and John Maynard Keynes. They stood on opposite sides of an intellectual fault line: Hayek believed in the supremacy of the market, while Keynes argued that governments would need to step in when markets failed.

Hayek was a radical economic liberal – he equated markets with freedom itself. Interference with markets by the state was an attack on freedom, which would lead to increasing political control and to totalitarianism. Hayek also defended markets on the grounds that they were a better way of coordinating individuals than any kind of central planning. People make decisions in an environment of uncertainty and on the basis of localized knowledge, and their behaviour influences prices, so the prices that emerge in markets are a distillation of all this disparate information about local conditions. In this way 'spontaneous order' emerges. Hayek argued that a central planner could never collect and interpret all this information.

Conspicuous consumption

Suppose that Jane buys a new coat. Standard economics assumes that Jane has a stable set of desires for goods and services – when properly satisfied these contribute to his well-being. He bought that particular coat because winter was drawing in and he liked the design. Jane's desire is self-contained: it is not connected to the judgements of others.

But if Jane had chosen an Armani coat in order to display his wealth to others, he would be engaging in what American economist Thorstein Veblen called conspicuous consumption. Now his desire for the coat is connected to other people's perception of it, namely that it tells them about Jane's own 'high status'. A status good has to be something that Jane can own, but others can't – as countries get richer and more people can afford Armani coats, Jane might have to start buying yachts in order to continue to communicate his status. Veblen argued that because of this, conspicuous consumption is wasteful.

Family economics

Economic analysis traditionally starts with the individual and the firm, but individuals are also members of families. Family economics uses economic principles to analyse people's decisions about marriage, having children and the distribution of resources within families. Marriage can allow people to pool resources, divide up their labour into different household tasks and share market risks. Different family members may have different preferences about how resources should be used. Studies have found settings in which mothers give greater weight to spending on children than fathers do. This drives policy initiatives in developing countries aimed at giving mothers greater control of family resources: it is hoped that these enhance the nutrition and education of children. Family economics also studies fertility behaviour, distinguishing between child 'quantity' and 'quality'. If there is a high future return to education, parents may have fewer children but spend more on their education, choosing quality over quantity. Broader changes in the economy can alter this trade-off.

Microcredit projects in developing countries frequently focus on offering small loans that allow women to start up businesses, based on the idea that mothers are more likely to invest wisely.

Gender

Standard economics says little about gender: economies consist of interactions between firms and rational, genderless individuals. Recently, however, some economists have begun to consider the role of gender in more detail. They argue that the usual starting point of 'rational economic man' can't address the discrimination and power imbalances faced by women. What's more, existing ways of measuring the economy don't properly take the contribution of women into account. Women carry out a lot of work within households, caring for children and relatives, cooking and cleaning, and so on. Because this work is usually not paid for in a formal economic transaction, it is not counted in national income. Macroeconomic policies can also affect men and women differently: cutbacks often hit women hardest, especially if health or education cuts increase their responsibilities in the home. GDP is only a partial measure of economic progress, the critics argue: human well-being is dependent on a broad range of factors, including the position of women in society.

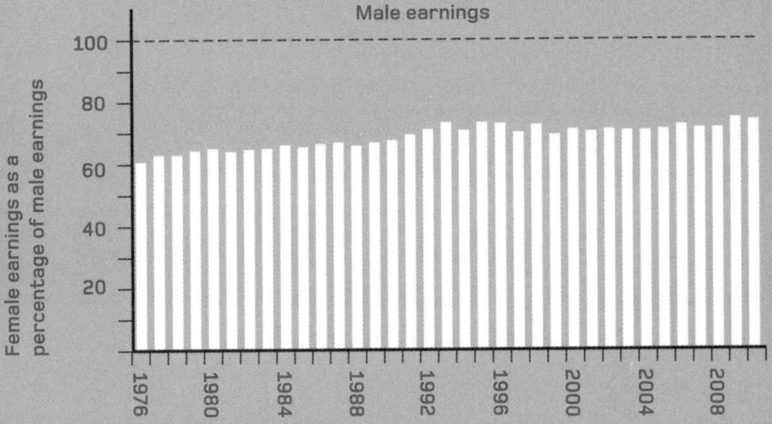

Over time, female earnings have lagged behind male earnings, as shown in this graph of earnings ratios in Canada from 1976–2011.

Social capital

Traditionally, when economists talk about capital they mean physical things – conveyor belts, electricity pylons, lathes – that along with labour can be used to produce goods. More recently, however, economists have begun to talk about social capital – broadly speaking, the connections between individuals that create social networks and trust. Like machines, social capital acts as an input into production, with large amounts of social capital allowing for more economic activity.

The market exchange and information sharing that make up economic life depend on social capital: without trust, even the most basic economic activity would be difficult. Belonging to social networks allows individuals to learn about market opportunities and jobs, and to coordinate with each other. Economists have tried to measure social capital and link it to national economic fortunes, but the idea can also be criticized: some argue that it is a hopelessly vague concept that cannot provide a robust explanation of economic performance.

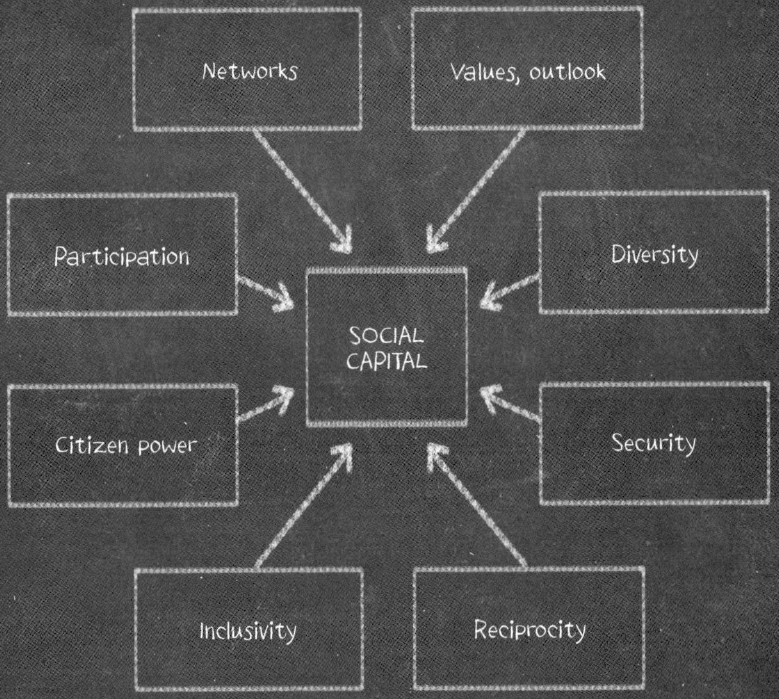
Networks
Values, outlook
Participation
Diversity
SOCIAL CAPITAL
Citizen power
Security
Inclusivity
Reciprocity

Economic reform

Economic activity can take place in all sorts of economic systems, from free market to state-run to communist. Economic reform includes a host of actions by governments to change, and hopefully improve, the nature of their economic systems. A famous example is the 'shock therapy' reform that followed the fall of communism in Eastern Europe, in which countries were rapidly subjected to market forces. African nations, too, underwent similar reforms. These changes had mixed results, and later reform programmes have broadened to encompass changes in the legal and political institutions required for markets to work. Even advantageous reforms can get derailed – they often threaten the privileges of politically powerful people, such as industrialists who might lose from opening up to international competition. The distribution of costs and benefits from a valuable reform may not be known, so to minimize the risk of ending up on the losing side people may oppose it. Such problems make economic reform one of the most complex and uncertain types of government action.

Growth and the sources of growth

One of the founders of economics, Adam Smith, entitled his magnum opus *The Wealth of Nations*, and the differences that make some countries rich and others poor remain a major preoccupation of the discipline. Today, economists wrestle with the problem by searching for the causes of growth.

Growth is simply the rate of expansion in a country's output. Over time, even small differences in this rate can lead to big gaps in living standards: over 30 years a country growing at 4 per cent per year would be one-third richer than one starting from the same point but growing at just 3 per cent. For poor countries, a small growth disparity might make the difference between having the resources to immunize children against diseases or not. In simple terms, economies grow when more inputs – capital, labour and skills – are put into production, and when new technologies make the inputs more productive. Understanding how this happens, and why it happens more easily in some countries than others, is a holy grail of economics.

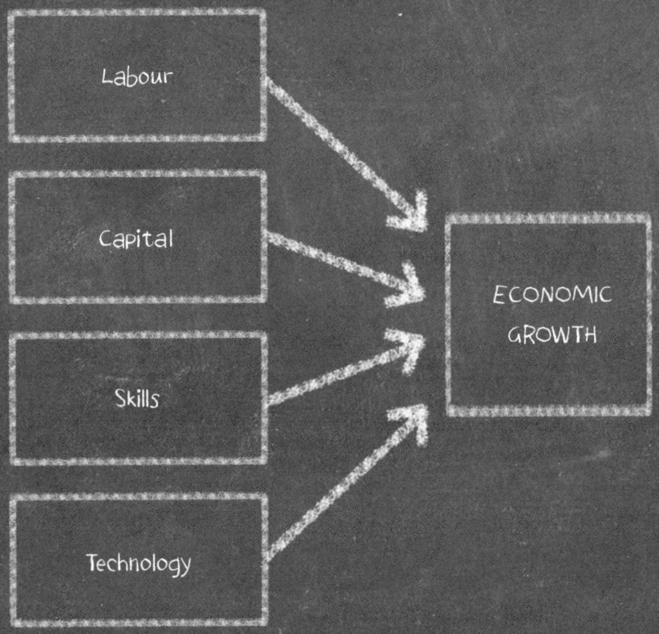
Labour
Capital
Skills
Technology
ECONOMIC
GROWTH

Living standards and productivity

Living standards rise when economies become more productive. Suppose that a new technology allows workers to produce more each day: the economy generates more resources to go round, wages rise and living standards improve. Productivity improvements can be driven by the capital and labour available in a country. Suppose that a country is scarce in labour compared to capital – wages are high, but the prices of machines and fuel are low. This will encourage businesses to install machines, and as these machines are improved, the economy becomes more productive. Some argue that this is what happened during Britain's Industrial Revolution.

Another factor behind productivity improvement is market size. When markets are large, cost advantages can be reaped through the mass production of standardized products, a factor that was critical to the early growth of the American economy. Competition, too, helps productivity – when firms are in competition they look for ways of being more productive.

Economic convergence

In the mid-1950s, American economist Robert Solow devised a theory of economic growth which predicts that over time countries' living standards converge: poor countries will catch up with the rich. The idea is that the lower starting point of poor countries actually allows them to grow faster. When a country has little capital – factories, roads and machines – extra investment has a big impact on growth. When a country is rich and already has a large capital stock, the same extra investment has a much smaller impact on growth. Over time, then, as countries get richer they grow more slowly.

Like all theories, Solow's depends on simplifying assumptions – a crucial one is that all countries have access to the same stock of technology. In practice, there are all sorts of economic, political and social barriers to accessing the latest technologies. Some countries, such as South Korea and other Asian nations have managed to catch up with the industrialized West, but for many convergence remains a chimera.

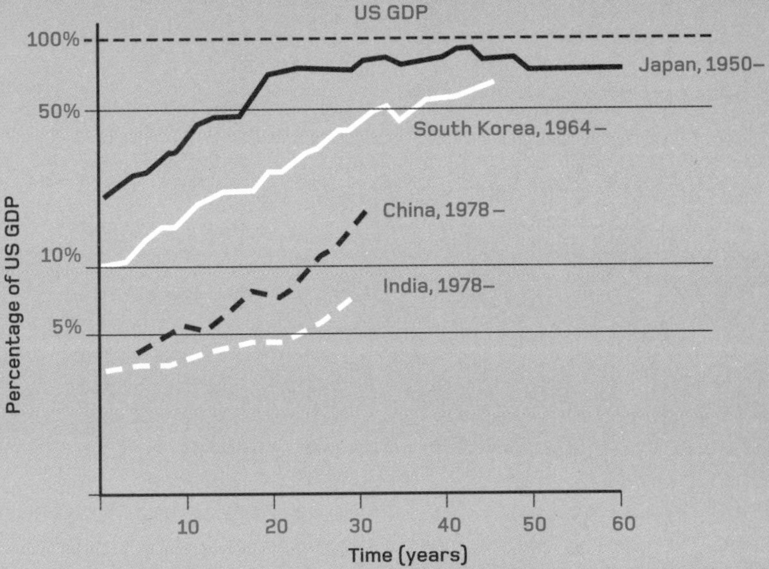

A graph of post-war GDP per head in several Asian economies shows how growth is fastest in the early years of development, and then tends to flatten out, allowing other countries to catch up.

Endogenous growth

In early growth theories, economists assumed that the technological progress that helps generate long-run economic growth came from outside of the economy: growth was said to be 'exogenous'. In the mid-1980s, a new wave of theories argued that technology was generated by forces within the economy, and hence that growth was 'endogenous'.

Under the older approach, all countries have access to the same exogenous technology. Because extra capital investment has less of an impact the more capital a country has, growth slows down as countries develop, so poorer countries tend to catch up with richer ones. Endogenous theory weakens this conclusion – here, technology is recognized as coming from innovation that is influenced by economic incentives. New technology and knowledge produced by one firm can help the productivity of others. This can offset the diminishing impact of capital as economies get richer, so growth doesn't necessarily have to slow down.

Investment in improved technologies such as automated production lines allows growth to continue in rich countries.

Technology

Technological change is critical to raising living standards over the long run. Improvements in technology allow a greater volume and variety of goods to be produced, although some worry that new technology causes unemployment if mechanization makes labour obsolete. In fact, by making each worker more productive, technology can increase the demand for labour. It can even create entirely new sectors of the economy, bringing with them new employment opportunities.

Some 'general purpose technologies', such as electricity, are revolutionary: they raise the productivity of every sector of the economy. Other kinds of technological improvement – for example, more efficient ovens – raise productivity in specific sectors. The introduction of a new general purpose technology is a leap that fundamentally transforms economies and can lead to new patterns of economic growth. In the 18th and 19th centuries that leap arose from steam power, while today it is coming from information and communication technologies.

BU9348
021

Population growth

Modern concerns about our planet's capacity to support an ever-rising population hark back to the prediction of English demographer Thomas Malthus in the 18th century that England's prosperity was threatened by population growth. He argued that higher living standards could never be sustained. Firstly, they would cause a lower death rate because people would be better nourished. Secondly, they would allow people to have more children. The result would be an ever-increasing population. With more people on a fixed amount of land, food production would not be able to keep up and living standards would decline, dooming people to subsistence or worse.

Of course, Malthus's prediction didn't come to pass, because technological improvements in England allowed more food to be produced so that both living standards *and* population grew. Today, some very poor countries do seem to be caught in a Malthusian trap in which higher population translates into poverty. However, the richest nations exited it long ago.

Industrialization and modern growth

On the path to high growth and advanced development, countries inevitably industrialize, moving away from largely rural, agricultural societies. The Russian economist Simon Kuznets summarized the set of economic and social changes that this involves in the term 'modern economic growth'.

Societies undergoing this form of growth see rising living standards alongside a growing population: higher population no longer means lower income. The driver is 'structural transformation': workers move from fields and family firms to big companies and factories in the cities. The share of industrial production in national income starts to rise, accompanied by broader cultural trends such as secularization. Britain achieved modern economic growth with the Industrial Revolution of the 18th and 19th centuries. European nations, the United States and others followed soon after. However, many countries have yet to make the transition and an explanation of the precise factors that trigger it remains elusive.

Creative destruction

The term 'creative destruction' encapsulates the insight that the progress of capitalism is bumpy – to create anew, the old has to be destroyed. The Austrian economist Joseph Schumpeter argued that economic development is powered by entrepreneurs who innovate and take risks. Entrepreneurs come up with new products and create markets for them. Think, perhaps, of the laptop or the compact disc player – unprecedented products whose inventors created with no guarantees of success. The firm that introduces a new product earns high profit for a time – the promise of this return is what drives the innovative effort – but eventually other firms start to produce similar products and the market plateaus.

In this way of thinking, recessions are necessary to weed out old, stagnant businesses and make way for a new generation of entrepreneurs. This is different from the standard economic view of the market's 'invisible hand' (see page 44) smoothly allocating resources to the best possible uses.

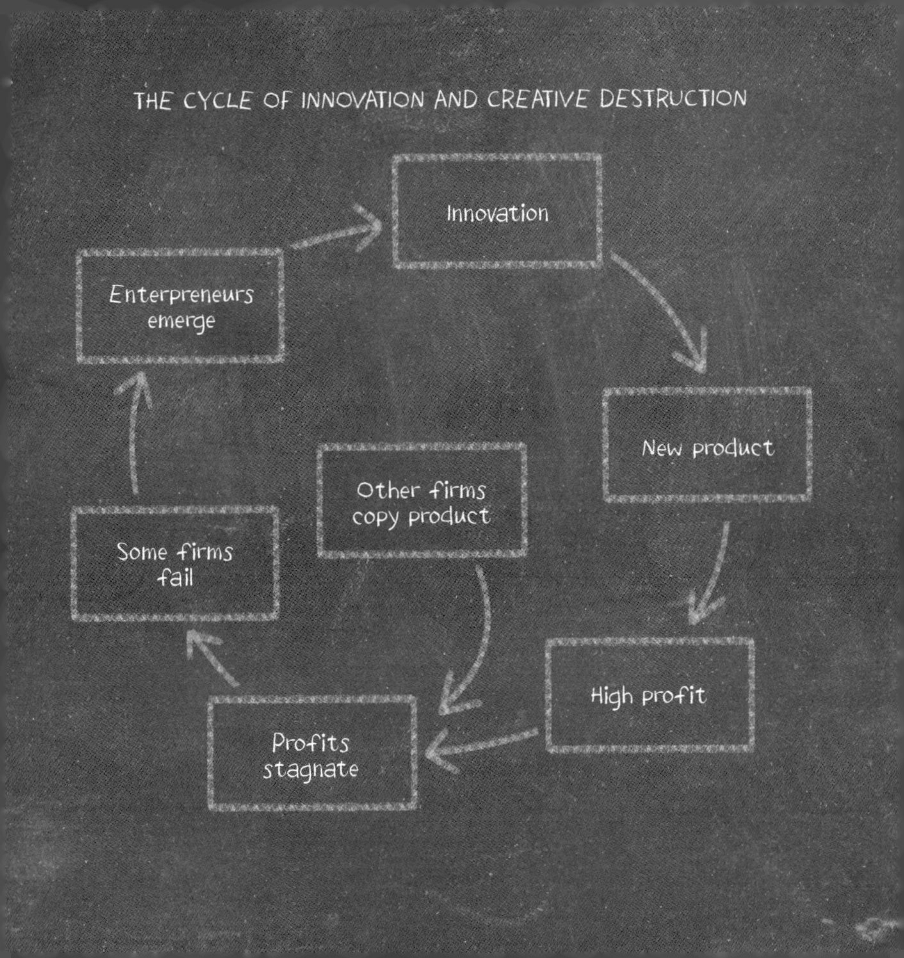
THE CYCLE OF INNOVATION AND CREATIVE DESTRUCTION
Innovation
New product
High profit
Other firms copy product
Profits stagnate
Some firms fail
Enterpreneurs emerge

Development economics

Development economics is the study of how the economies of poor countries function, and how they might become richer. Some economists question whether there are really fundamental differences in the economic laws governing poor and rich countries, but others believe the problems facing poor countries are so specific that special theories are required. An early idea was that poor economies needed a 'big push'. A new port might only help trade if a road was built, but for the road to be worthwhile it would have to lead somewhere like a port. This circularity could only be broken if the state coordinated a range of simultaneous and complementary investments – something private markets would be unable to do. By the 1970s, this view began to fall out of favour – economists argued that too much state and not enough market hobbled developing economies. In the 1980s, the World Bank and International Monetary Fund brought in free market reforms. These, too, had patchy results, and attention has now turned to the challenge of encouraging states to function better.

Poverty lines

One way of measuring the degree of poverty in a society is to define a minimum level of income below which a person is said to be in poverty. One example of such a 'poverty line' is the often-cited dollar-a-day, but how should a poverty line be set? Economists are more concerned with well-being or 'utility' than with money itself, so one might try to define a line that delivers some basic level of utility, perhaps by using subjective measures of well-being. An alternative approach is to use a more objective criterion, such as a minimum calorie level.

An important distinction is between relative and absolute poverty: while an absolute line might be set according to a biological criterion, a relative measure is stated as a minimum proportion of average income. With a relative income line, there will always be some people living in poverty, even if they own televisions and mobile phones. Poverty lines have their drawbacks, however: increased deprivation among those far below the poverty line doesn't register in a higher poverty rate.

Entitlement theory and famines

It is often believed that famines are caused by shortages of food such as those following harvest failures. In the early 1980s, Indian economist Amartya Sen developed his entitlement theory, showing that the causes of famines are in fact more complex. In this theory, 'entitlements' are the set of goods and services that households are able to obtain either through producing them, buying them or receiving them from the government. Even in poor countries many people do not produce their own food – they earn wages which they use to buy food, and the balance of wages against the price of food largely determines their entitlements to food. Famines can occur when entitlements fall below the minimum amount of food needed to survive. This can be caused by falling wages or rising prices, rather than by actual reductions in local food production. This is what happened in a famine in Bengal in the 1940s where wages fell behind food inflation – the price trends were more important than changes in overall food supply.

Debt relief

During the latter decades of the 20th century, many poor nations amassed huge amounts of debt. Such debt becomes a problem when growth is insufficient to generate the resources needed to repay, and by the 1990s, with a large debt burden alongside poor economic performance, many nations were unable to meet their interest payments. Debt relief was a large-scale cancellation and rescheduling of debts in response to these countries' economic crises. Many economists argued that Western nations and international organizations that made the loans should cancel them. The debts were so large that repaying them in full would require cuts to essential investments needed for development. Cutting the debts would help these nations grow. Another case for debt relief was that many of the debt obligations were taken on by earlier corrupt or illegitimate regimes – should post-apartheid South Africa have to pay the debts of the apartheid government? However, debt relief has not been without its critics: some say that it rewards bad policy and corruption.

Debt relief is aimed at enabling poor countries to spend money on schools rather than interest payments.

Dependency theory

Most economists believe that trade between countries is 'win-win'. Dependency theory, which emerged after the Second World War, was a radical alternative approach. Its central idea was that trade between developed and developing countries is inherently unequal and exploitative. Rich countries buy raw materials from poor countries to fuel manufacturing, producing goods that are traded mainly with other developed nations. Investment in poor countries by rich ones tends to exploit rather than develop the local economy, it is argued. A related idea is that the 'terms of trade' – the imports a country can buy with its exports – often move against poor countries as the prices of raw materials fall relative to those of manufactured goods. Dependency theorists argue that the result is a 'core' of ever richer industrialized nations alongside a 'periphery' of marginalized ones falling further behind. The rise of the 'Asian Tiger' economies (see page 400), has perhaps put paid to the dependency story, or at least suggested that there are important caveats.

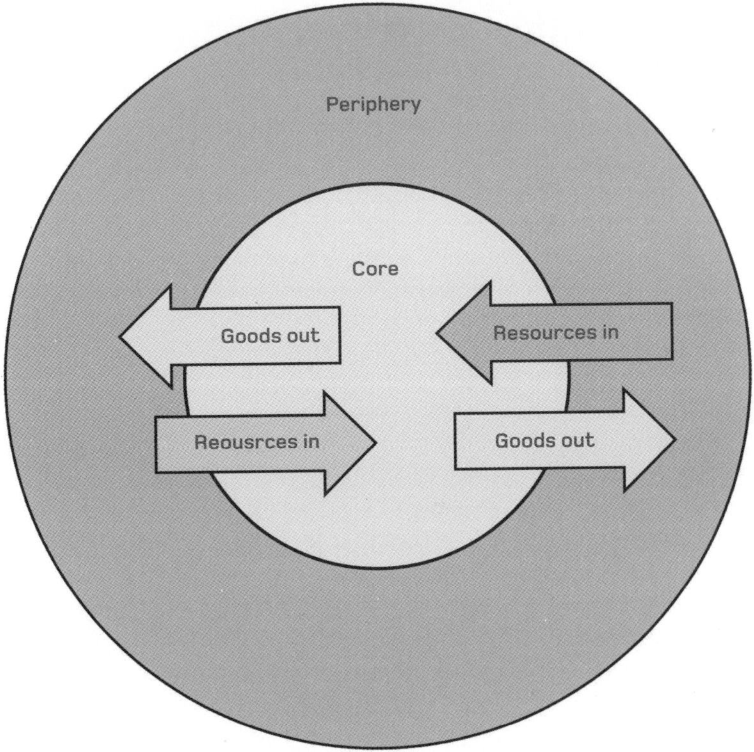
Periphery
Core
Goods out
Resources in
Reousrces in
Goods out

Inequality and growth

The links between growth and inequality have engrossed economists and fired popular debate. One view is that economic development implies rising inequality: when industries emerge in predominantly agricultural countries, inequality rises at first, because the new sectors offer higher wages but only make up a fraction of the economy. Others have argued that in the latter half of the 20th century economic growth drove the reduction of poverty and reduced inequality.

A different way of looking at things is to consider how the level of inequality itself affects economic performance. Some economists have suggested that inequality stifles economic growth. Inequality means that the capital stock is in the hands of an elite. The mass of the population, who own no capital, want a high rate of tax to fund public services. Because they form the electoral majority, governments end up placing a high rate of tax on capital, but because growth is reliant on the accumulation of capital, this actually slows the rate of growth.

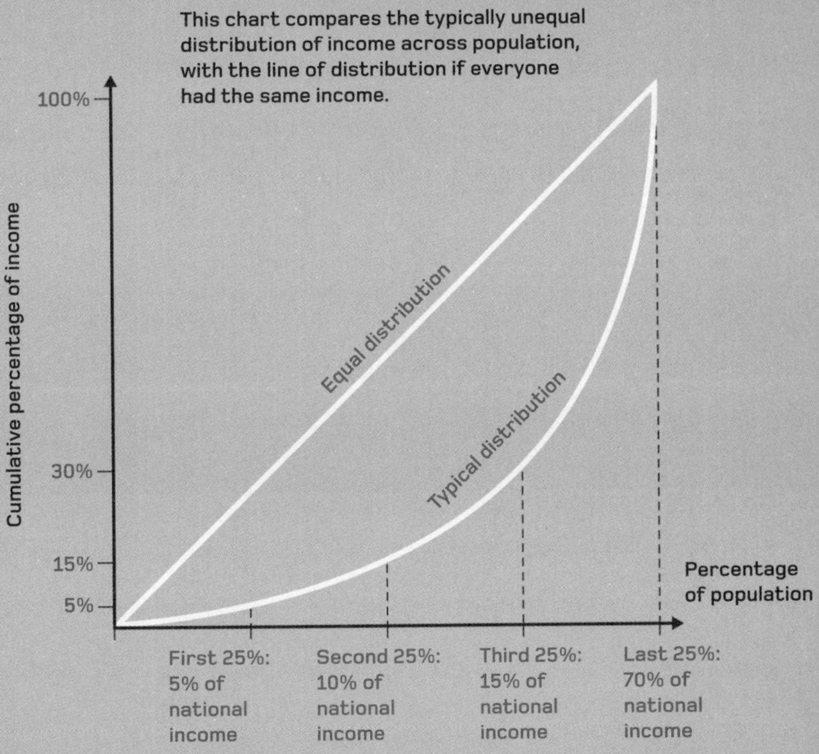
This chart compares the typically unequal distribution of income across population, with the line of distribution if everyone had the same income.
Cumulative percentage of income
100%
30%
15%
5%
Equal distribution
Typical distribution
Percentage of population
First 25%: 5% of national income
Second 25%: 10% of national income
Third 25%: 15% of national income
Last 25%: 70% of national income

Human capital

Capital is made up of goods such as machines and factories, investment in which allows future output of products and services. Economics has extended this idea from physical capital to human beings. Human capital is the productive capacity of people – the skills and aptitudes that allow them to drive tractors, design skyscrapers and draw up balance sheets.

Just as a firm builds up its physical capital by installing new machines, people invest in their human capital by undertaking education and training. A firm buys a new machine if it will earn a return in the future, and similarly, workers invest in education if it is rewarded with a higher wage. Workers get paid a wage equal to the extra amount of production they create. Hence, because more human capital makes them more productive, employers will be willing to pay them more. The gap in wages between skilled and unskilled workers is known as the skill premium. Human capital is needed for economic growth, and a lack of it can seriously hamper economic development.

The Asian Tigers

One of the most dramatic economic developments of the 20th century was the transformation of the so-called Asian Tigers – Hong Kong, South Korea, Singapore and Taiwan – from marginal economies into advanced, developed nations with standards of living to match those in Europe and the United States. Some contend that their success was due to the state getting out of the way and allowing free markets to operate. Others argue that these countries had 'developmental states' – governments that deviated from orthodox recommendations to provide only basic public goods and not to meddle with the markets. This second explanation stresses the authoritarian, interventionist nature of these governments, which although embracing markets, also shaped them – for example, by directing production towards particular industrial sectors. Whatever the truth, it is certainly the case that these countries had unique kinds of economic organization. More recently, China's economy has also taken off. It, too, has crafted its own mix of state intervention and market incentives.

The informal economy

Like grass between paving stones, economic life sprouts among the cracks in the formal economic sector of private companies and state bureaucracies. Pedlars hawking bric-a-brac from makeshift stalls, shoeshine boys and even currency black marketeers all make up what has come to be known as an informal economy. Such economies have emerged in many eras, and still exist in a wide range of societies.

Recently, there has been interest in the informal sectors of developing nations. In such countries, the informal economy makes up a large share of economic activity. Because it is not part of the formal structure of legal regulation and taxation it is hard to measure. The urban populations of many developing countries have swelled as rural migrants arrive looking for work, and many of these people end up in the informal sector. Some development policy is aimed at helping people in this part of the economy – for example, by providing them with loans, which they would otherwise be unable to obtain from banks.

Exhaustible resources

Exhaustible resources are those whose stocks are finite, such as coal and oil – with continual use they will run out. Economically, exhaustible resources are like financial assets: one theory says that the profit (price minus cost) of an exhaustible resource should rise at a rate equal to the interest rate. If the profit from oil were to rise slower than this, then oilfield owners would pump and sell their entire stock, putting the revenues into a bank to earn interest. This would reduce today's price so that given future prices, profits would grow again at the rate of interest. Hence, the price of an exhaustible resource should gradually rise as it gets used up. But instead, prices of natural resources have often shown long-term falls.

Commonly, the point at which a resource is going to be used up is unknown, and technological advances that allow for more efficient extraction or use of the resource can push this point further into the future. Perhaps the real unknown, though, is whether such deferral faces an ultimate limit.

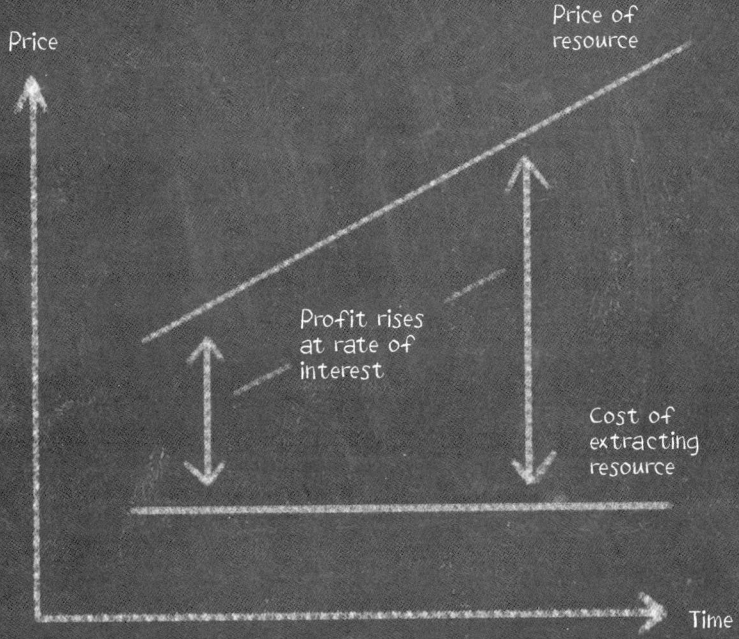

Price
Price of
resource
Profit rises
at rate of
interest
Cost of
extracting
resource
Time

The environment and collective action

With climate change, the world faces a gigantic collective action problem. Imagine a business in Spain which produces greenhouse gases. It might limit emissions if they reduce its own profits, but like other businesses, it will not take into account the impact of its emissions on other firms, whether Spanish, French or German. Another aspect of the collective action problem is that protection of the environment is what economists call a 'public good' (see page 58), and raises the question of why one should contribute to the costs of protection when one can free ride on the efforts of others. For climate change, the problem is acute because the greatest costs will be borne in the future rather than the present. One solution is to set pollution quotas, although these are hard to enforce. Another is to tax pollution. Carbon-trading schemes attempt to create a market for pollution, forcing firms to face the full costs of their pollution production. This allows firms who can easily cut emissions to make the biggest reductions.

Glossary

Balance of payments
A record of the transactions between residents of one country and those of other countries, including imports and exports of goods and services and capital flows, such as investments and loans.

Barter
The direct exchange of goods – the trading of a fish for a tomato, for example – without the use of money. Barter is less efficient than exchange using money, since it requires that both parties have access to tradable goods.

Bond
A financial security issued by a company or government in order to raise money. The buyer of the bond lends money to the issuer in exchange for interest payments.

Capital
Goods for production, such as machines and factories, that are used to make goods for consumption, such as tinned soup and shoes.

Competition
Situations in which firms compete for buyers with many other firms, driving down prices and profits.

Consumption
Spending on goods in order to directly satisfy the desires of individuals. Spending on a restaurant meal is consumption, whereas the restaurant's purchase of a new oven is not.

Cost
The amount of money that a firm needs to spend to produce a certain level of output. Costs include expenditure on raw materials and labour.

Debt
Money that is owed by a borrower to a lender. Debts can be incurred

by individuals, firms and governments.

Deflation
The opposite of inflation, deflation is a situation in which the general level of prices in an economy is falling.

Demand
The amount of a good or service that buyers are willing to purchase at a particular price. Usually, demand rises when the price falls, but there are exceptions to this pattern.

Direct tax
A tax that is levied on the person who pays it, such as taxes on employees' incomes, and which is paid directly to the tax authority.

Division of labour
The separation of a production process into steps, each of which is carried out by specialized workers. Division of labour is an important element of modern production methods.

Exchange rates
The price of one currency such as the British pound, in relation to another, such as the US dollar.

Fiscal policy
The setting of levels of taxation and spending by the government in order to influence the level of demand in the economy, and the distribution of income.

Gross Domestic Product (GDP)
The total value of goods and services produced in a country over a year – a common measure of national income.

Human capital
The economically productive capacity of people. Human capital can be enhanced through training and education.

Indirect tax
A tax imposed on goods that are purchased, as opposed to direct taxes on earned income.

Inflation
Increase in the general level of prices – that is, increases in the prices of many goods and services.

Investment
Expenditure on capital goods, such as machines, which are in turn used to make other goods, such as those ultimately purchased by consumers. Firms make investments in order to expand and renew their stock of capital.

Marginal cost
The extra cost incurred by a firm as a result of a small increase in production.

Marginal revenue
The extra revenue earned by a firm as a result of a small increase in sales of its good.

Monetary policy
Actions taken by governments or central banks to influence the amount of money in the economy.

Monopoly
A firm that is the only supplier of a good or service. Monopolists are able to charge higher prices because of the lack of competition.

Oligopoly
A market that is dominated by a handful of large firms, whose decisions may therefore have an influence on each other beyond the normal laws of the market.

Opportunity cost
The cost of an option in terms of the next best alternative. For example, the opportunity cost of investment in new hospital equipment might be computers for a school that could have been bought instead.

Productivity
The efficiency with which raw materials are made into goods. Productivity is higher when more can be produced with less.

Profit
The excess of revenue over costs, and the goal of profit-maximizing firms.

Recession
A period of declining economic output, usually coinciding with rising unemployment and falling prices.

Revenue
The amount of money a firm earns from selling some quantity of its goods.

Saving
Income that is not spent on goods and services, but is instead preserved for anticipated future spending.

Share
Part ownership in a firm. Shares in public companies are traded on stock exchanges, and offer rights to a say in a firm's management and a share in its profits.

Supply
The amount of a good or service that firms are willing to supply at a particular price. Usually, supply rises when prices increase.

Tariff
Taxes imposed on imports. These raise revenue for the government and reduce demand for foreign goods.

Index

Quercus Editions Ltd
55 Baker Street,
7th Floor, South Block
London
W1U 8EW

First published in 2014

Copyright © Quercus Editions Ltd 2014
Text by Niall Kishtainy
Illustrations by Tim Brown
Design and editorial: Pikaia imaging
Design assistant: Kathryn Brown

All rights reserved. No part of this publication may be reproduced, stored in a retrieval system, or transmitted in any form or by any means, electronic, mechanical, photocopying, recording, or otherwise, without the prior permission in writing of the copyright owner and publisher.

The picture credits constitute an extension to this copyright notice.

Every effort has been made to contact copyright holders. However, the publishers will be glad to rectify in future editions any inadvertent omissions brought to their attention.

Quercus Editions Ltd hereby exclude all liability to the extent permitted by law for any errors or omissions in this book and for any loss, damage or expense (whether direct or indirect) suffered by a third party relying on any information contained in this book.

A catalogue record of this book is available from the British Library

ISBN 978 1 78206 647 7

Printed and bound in China

10 9 8 7 6 5 4 3 2 1

Picture credits 2: Shutterstock/Everett Collection; 4–5: Shutterstock/SeanPavonePhoto; 9: © Ewing Galloway/ClassicStock/Corbis; 11: © Issei Kato/Reuters/Corbis; 17: Shutterstock/ml; 21: Shutterstock/Africa Studio; 31: © Franco Cogoli/SOPA RF/SOPA/Corbis; 33: Shutterstock/Africa Studio; 39: Shutterstock/Aigars Reinholds; 43: Shutterstock/connel; 55: Shutterstock/evronphoto; 59: Shutterstock/Sorbis; 63: Shutterstock/zentilia; 65: Shutterstock/Sashkin; 67: Shutterstock/Sakonboon Sansri; 69: Shutterstock/Oleksiy Mark; 73: Shutterstock/Uka; 77: Shutterstock/hxdbzxy; 79: Shutterstock/VladisChern; 81: Shutterstock/Ints Vikmanis; 87: Shutterstock/AMC Photography; 91: Shutterstock/2j architecture; 93: Shutterstock/Imagewell; 103: RIA Novosti archive, image #978776/Alexey Kudenko/CC-BY-SA 3.0; 109–10: Shutterstock/SeanPavonePhoto; 113: Shutterstock/Jim Pruitt; 117: Shutterstock/Everett Collection; 123: Shutterstock/gillmar; 131: Shutterstock/sixninepixels; 133: Shutterstock/PHB.cz (Richard Semik); 137: Shutterstock/Fer Gregory; 143: Shutterstock/Pavel L Photo and Video; 147: Mary Evans/Everett Collection; 155: Shutterstock/pollix; 159: by Ester Inbar, available from http://commons.wikimedia.org/wiki/User:ST; 161: Shutterstock/Southdown Studios; 163: Shutterstock/Kodda; 171: carlourossi via wikimedia; 175: Shutterstock/Arcady; 177: Shutterstock/Somchai Som; 181: Shutterstock/Luciano Mortula; 189: Shutterstock/Zurijeta; 191: Shutterstock/Radu Bercan; 193: Shutterstock/Paulo M. F. Pires; 199: Shutterstock/Everett Collection; 203: Shutterstock/Petrafler; 213: © Philimon Bulawayo/Reuters/Corbis; 217: Shutterstock/Yelena Panyukova; 223: Shutterstock/Dragana Gerasimoski; 235: © Kevin LaMarque/Reuters/Corbis; 241: © Hulton-Deutsch Collection/Corbis; 243: Shutterstock/Stephen Griffith; 245: Shutterstock/fritz16; 247: Shutterstock/PanicAttack; 249: Shutterstock/Petronilo G. Dangoy Jr.; 257: The Friedman Foundation for Educational Choice; 267: © Bettmann/CORBIS; 269: Shutterstock/r.nagy; 283: Shutterstock/David Fowler; 287: Topical Press Agency; 289: Shutterstock/Anna Tsekhmister; 293: Shutterstock/Leroy Harvey; 296: Shutterstock/Yuri Samsonov; 297: Shutterstock/shutter; 299: Shutterstock/jvd-wolf; 301: Shutterstock/Nick Pavlakis; 311: Shutterstock/E.G.Pors; 315: Shutterstock/Darrin Henry; 323: Shutterstock/CarpathianPrince; 325: Dorothea Lange U.S. Department of Agriculture; 327: Shutterstock/Vladimir Koletic; 331: Shutterstock/Lisa S.; 333: Bundesarchiv, Bild 102-12023/Georg Pahl/CC-BY-SA; 343: Shutterstock/archideaphoto; 345: Shutterstock/1000 Words; 353: Hulton Archive; 355: Shutterstock/godrick; 357: U.S. National Archives and Records Administration; 359: © UPP/TopFoto; 361: Shutterstock/Karkas; 363: Shutterstock/Tracing Tea; 369: © David Turnley/Corbis; 373: Shutterstock/BartlomiejMagierowski; 377: Shutterstock/Small Town Studio; 379: Shutterstock/Ragma Images; 381: Shutterstock/Vladimir Wrangel; 383: Shutterstock/Stokkete; 387: Shutterstock/joyfull; 389: Shutterstock/paul prescott; 393: Shutterstock/Pecold; 399: Shutterstock/Anneka; 401: Leeyan Kym N. Fontano; 403: Shutterstock/project1photography; 407: Shutterstock/Yvonne Pijnenburg-Schonewille.